The
ABUNDANT LIFE
BIBLE STUDY COURSE

By

RAY E. BAUGHMAN

Illustrated by Glenn Retzlaff

MOODY PRESS
CHICAGO

ISBN 0-8024-0047-7

42 Printing/LC/Year 88 87 86

Printed in the United States of America

INTRODUCTION

In John 10:10 Jesus said: "I am come that they might have *life,* and that they might have it *more abundantly.*" But most people have turned from Christ and rejected the gift of eternal life which He has offered. Just as sad is the fact that most people, who have received Him as Saviour and passed from death to life, are not living the *abundant life* and never have experienced it. The Bible describes this condition as being "babes in Christ" (I Corinthians 3:1).

This Bible study course has been written—

1. To introduce those to Christ who do not know Him as their Saviour.
2. To help Christians grow spiritually and possess this happy, joyful *abundant life* that Christ promised.
3. To help them in turn to share this life with others who have not had the privilege of meeting the Person, *the Lord Jesus Christ.*

INSTRUCTIONS

Work the lessons in order. Each lesson is based upon what has been discussed in the previous lessons. The lessons are divided into three main

3

parts: the lesson text, the questions, and the memory work plus a suggested Bible-reading program.

Read through the lesson text at least once before starting on the questions.

First *read* the question, then look up the reference in your Bible. Most of the questions will be: true or false; yes or no; completion, requiring one or two words;

multiple-choice in which the correct answer must be selected from several suggested answers; and matching questions in which a group of references and a group of answers will have to be properly matched. Start a loose-leaf notebook.

Write the answer in your notebook. Using the same procedure, go through all the questions and write your answers.

Start on the memory verses the same day you start on the lesson. Make your memory cards and go over the verses each day. This will not take long but it is very important. Many feel this is the most profitable part of the course. The secret of memorizing is review, *review, review!*

This study course has not only been designed for personal study, but also for the individual  soul winner or local church in its follow-up program through the use of individual counselors or "big brothers." This course can be used as a very effective contact with members of the Armed Forces or students who are away at school.

CONTENTS

MEETING CHRIST

Meet a very special Person, and become personally acquainted with Him. We know *of* the President of the United States, but very few of us have ever personally met him. We believe that he exists, and we know a lot of facts *about* him, but we do not actually know him.

Most people have heard of Jesus Christ. They know and believe certain facts about Him—His birth, His teachings, His death and resurrection, but they never have met Him in a personal way so He could become their Saviour and Lord.

AN EXAMPLE

Many people look to Jesus as the perfect example after which to pattern their lives. His life was perfect, without flaw, above reproach and unmarred by sin. Even the judge who con-

9

demned Him to death said, "I find no fault in him" (John 19:4). But every honest person must admit that even though the pattern is perfect he is unable to follow it. You must come to know Him as more than a good example.

A TEACHER OR PROPHET

While Jesus was on earth, great crowds came to hear Him speak and teach. The rich, the poor, the highly educated and the common people all recognized that Jesus was a great Teacher, that He was "come from God" (John 3:2). His cleverest enemies failed to trap Him with their questions. But Jesus told the ruler of the Jews in John 3:1-15 that he needed to know more about Him than the fact that He was a great Teacher or a Prophet.

A KING

The Sunday before Jesus died great crowds of people wanted to make Him their king. They were looking for someone to remove them from under the hand of Rome and restore their independence. But before they could know Him as King they needed to meet Him in a different way, as their Redeemer.

A MARTYR OR A HERO

Everyone admires a hero, or a person who is martyred for a good cause, but Christ's death was not just a horrible mistake or an accident. It was for this purpose that Christ came into the world—to die. It was planned before the world began (Acts 2:23; I Peter 1:20). Jesus could have called twelve legions of angels to help Him (Matthew 26:53). You must understand that Jesus is more than just a martyr.

As Saviour

Before you can meet Christ as your Saviour, you must understand four things.

Man was originally created for the glory of God (Isaiah 43:7). But this original purpose was interrupted by sin, and man became very evil and unprofitable (Romans 3:10-12). Now the sentence of death is over all men for "all have sinned" (Romans 3:23); "for the wages of sin is death" (Romans 6:23); and the sentence is already upon us (John 3:18). So—

1. You need to be saved.
2. You cannot save yourself; salvation is a free gift (Ephesians 2:8, 9; Titus 3:5; Romans 6:23).
3. Christ has purchased salvation for you. Christ has paid the penalty as your Substitute: "Who his own self bare our sins in his own body on the tree" (I Peter 2:24); "Christ hath redeemed us from the curse of the law, being made a curse for us" (Galatians 3:13; Isaiah 53:6).
4. *You must believe and receive Jesus as your Saviour.*

This is the way in which you must know Him. Jesus said: "Behold, I stand at the door, and knock: if *any man* hear my voice, and open the door, I will come in to him" (Revelation 3:20); "But as many as received him, to them gave he power to become the sons of God, even to them that believe on his name" (John 1:12).

If you will receive Him and the saving work which He has performed for you, then you also receive eternal life, for eternal life is *in Him*, the Son of God (John 3:16; I John 5:11-13).

You can know and understand all these things but it will not help until you receive Him by faith into your heart.

QUESTIONS

1. The great purpose of the Bible is to give a history of the world (John 20:31). *Check true or false.*   T ☐   F ☐

2. In John 8:12 Peter is called the light of the world.   T ☐   F ☐

3. All men are willing to come to the light of Jesus (John 3:19).   T ☐   F ☐

4. Those who do evil are afraid that their evil deeds will be reproved (John 3:20).   T ☐   F ☐

5. If a man sins he is a servant of sin (John 8:34).   T ☐   F ☐

6. Jesus said in John 16:9 that not believing on Him is a sin. T □ F □

7. All men are sinners (Rom. 3:23) T □ F □

8. The result of sin is death (Ezek 18:4; Rom. 6:23). T □ F □

9. The sinner is not under condemnation now but will be when he dies (John 3:18). T □ F □

10. Christ came to condemn you (John 3:17). T □ F □

11. Even though man is sinful God loves him (John 3:16). T □ F □

12. Because Christ died for everyone He will automatically save everyone (John 8:24). T □ F □

13. Jesus was proved guilty of several faults at His trial (John 19:4; Heb. 4:15). T □ F □

14. "For Christ also hath once suffered for sins, the just for the unjust [*your name* _____], that he might _____ us to God" (I Peter 3:18). "Who his own self bare our [*your name* _____] sins in his own body on the tree." (I Peter 2:24).

15. Romans 6:23 teacnes eternal life is a _____ _____

16. You receive it by doing more good things than bad things (Eph. 2:8, 9; Titus 3:5). T □ F □

17. What are your "righteousnesses" (good works)
like in God's sight (Isa. 64:6) ? _____

18. Could there be another way to God (Prov.
14:12; John 14:6; Acts 4:12) ? _____

19. Jesus says: "Behold, I stand at the door, and
knock: if any man hear my voice, and open
the door, I will _____ to him"
(Rev. 3:20).

20. "But as many as received him, to them gave
he power to become the sons of God, even to
them [your name _____] that believe
on his name" (John 1:12).

21. If you say, "I'll take my place as a sinner, for
all have sinned (Rom. 3:23) ; I turn to Christ,
the One who died in my place (I Peter 3:18) ;
and receive Jesus as my personal Saviour"
(John 1:12), will He save you? _____

22. Have you received Him? _____
When? _____

23. Do you believe He has saved you (John 5:24) ?
_____

24. To whom did Thomas speak just after he believed (John 20:28, 29)? _____

25. Whom should you thank after you believe?
_____ Have you? _____

26. What did Jesus tell the man in Mark 5:19 to
do? _____
Will you do the same? _____

LESSON 2

LIFE HAS BEGUN

The angels are rejoicing.—Luke 15:10

 For a new "babe" has been *born again* into the kingdom of God, for to the best of your knowledge you have received Jesus Christ as your personal Saviour.

If—this is true, then the Bible says that you have been *born of God* (John 1:12, 13). If you have not received Him, you should stop now and take this step. Do not try to "play Christian."

You have been born into the wealthiest family in the universe. You have become *heir* to many wonderful privileges and possessions, not only in this age but in the age to come (I Peter 1:3, 4).

It is important to remember that regardless of your position or training in the world, you are a spiritual "babe." Your present concern should be growth (I Peter 2:2, 3; I Corinthians 3:1).

In the following studies you will try to discover, to claim, to put to use, and to share your inheritance. Just as an heir often must wait until he is twenty-one years old, you will find that you must "grow up" spiritually before you can claim all your privileges.

It is not houses and lands, education and occupation, or the future wife and grandchildren of the new baby that concern the parents at his birth, but several important immediate needs.

PROTECTION FROM DISEASE

Doctors and nurses try very hard to protect a new baby from germs. You also must be guarded against the attacks of Satan. He has become very angry at losing a member of his kingdom, so now he will try to make your life a bad example before the world. Satan likes to see sinful, defeated Christians.

SHOTS

 Doctors know certain diseases exist and they give shots to children while they are still healthy, so the germs may be counteracted if contacted.

WARNING

You will be most sensitive to diseases that will hinder your spiritual growth in the first few days and weeks. Many a Christian's life has been stunted during this period.

THE DISEASE OF DOUBT

Satan usually attacks first with doubts. The main thought he will try to plant is that God is not good.

THE SYMPTOMS

Safety

A baby needs to feel secure and safe and loved. Satan will attempt to discredit the work that God has performed in your life. He will whisper to you, "You don't think that you are saved just by believing and receiving Jesus as your Saviour? You will need to do more than that to have your sins blotted out and to get to Heaven." *What can you do?* See what God says, and stand on *His* promises.

What does God promise? I John 5:11, 12: "And this is the record, that God hath given to us eternal life, and this life is in his Son. He that hath the Son hath life; and he that hath not the Son of God hath not life." This is the first of four verses you should commit to memory. The thought of the effort involved to do this may be as distasteful to you as shots to a child. However, you will soon see the value of hiding the Word in your heart (Ps. 119:11), as you use the sword of the Spirit to meet the attacks of Satan.

Too Weak

Satan soon counters with the thought, O.K., so you have life, but you cannot live the way you should. What about *THIS* sin (as he brings a sin to your remembrance). You cannot quit that? God will expect too much of you. Why not give up now? It is no use trying; you are too weak. Again, rely upon God's promise, His faithfulness. I Corinthians 10:13: "There hath no temptation taken you but such as is common to man: but God is faithful, who will not suffer you to be tempted above that ye are able; but will with the temptation also make a way to escape, that ye may be able to bear it." (Carry these verses with you. Use spare minutes to go over them.)

Trouble

Just as little children often stray off and fall into the mud, even so Christians sometimes fall into sin. Satan, never missing an opportunity, is quick with the thought, Now you have done it. A holy God won't have anything to do with you now. Christians don't act that way. But just as a loving parent will pick up his crying child and clean the mud from his hands, even so we have a wonderful promise from our heavenly Father.

What does God say? I John 1:9: "If we confess our sins, he is faithful and just to forgive us our sins, and to cleanse us from all unrighteousness" (I John 1:9).

Care

A baby is very helpless. Parents must do and provide almost everything for him. So in order to meet Satan's accusation that God is not good we have this precious promise to stand on. John 16:24: "Hitherto have ye asked nothing in my name: ask, and ye shall receive, that your joy may be full" (John 16:24).

Claim this verse by asking God to help you memorize His Word. Repeat the reference at the *beginning and end* each time you practice to help fix it in your mind. The secret of memorizing is *review*.

To a large extent how fast you grow spiritually will depend upon YOUR attitude.

WHAT CAN A BABY DO?

There are three main things a new baby can do—cry, eat and sleep.

CRYING

You now have the privilege of crying unto God the Father, in the name of God the Son, Jesus Christ. Up until this time your prayers have been hindered (Isaiah 59:1, 2; John 9:31). Whether you realized it or not, you were in the terrible position of pushing aside with scorn the greatest gift God had—His Son (John 3:16); and then attempting to reach by Him to ask for selfish desires, or petty favors, or to try to bargain with God. *Now* you are on praying ground. "Ask, and it shall be given you" (Matthew 7:7, 8). For now you are asking in the name of God the Son and at His request (John 16:24).

EATING

Just as a baby needs food, so you need *spiritual food*. You would not think of waiting till Sunday and just dishing out a helping of whatever happened to be in the refrigerator, and then inviting the baby back next week for the next meal. Or saying, "If you get hungry before then, just walk into the kitchen and fix yourself a snack." In the first place he would be helpless; he couldn't walk or know what was in the cans; and if he did find something the chances are he could not digest it. No, a baby needs a special diet and a feeding schedule so he may grow properly. Likewise, spiritual "babes" to grow properly have certain needs that must be met.

FIRST FEEDING FORMULA

The Milk of the Word

"As newborn babes, desire the sincere milk of the word, that ye may grow thereby" (I Peter 2:2). With this lesson is a reading chart. Start feeding on the Word by reading the Gospel of John; then go to I and II Peter. Be sure you mark your chart each time you finish reading, and write the date beside each book when you finish it. Decide to read a portion every day (I Timothy 4:13; Revelation 1:3).

"Faith cometh by hearing, and hearing by the word of God" (Romans 10:17). Resolve to start your new life right by attending a Bible-believing church the very first Sunday after receiving Jesus as Saviour.

"That I might not sin against *thee*" (Psalm 119:11, 16). Continue to work on the verses on the cards in the memory pack.

Check the following: With God's help I will if at all possible—

1. Read a portion from His Word each day.
   _____

2. Attend a Bible-believing church Sunday.
   _____

3. Memorize the four verses this week. _____

4. Finish the answer sheets on Lessons 1 and 2 this week. _____

SLEEPING

A new baby spends much of his time sleeping. Several things must happen if he gets the needed rest. He must be fed the proper diet, and his body must digest the food. Often you need to be spiritually "burped" to remove the little problems that arise, so the Word may be spiritually digested and go out into your life as you grow in the Lord. But besides this a baby needs to feel loved and safe. This is expressed in the saying, "Safe as a baby in its mother's arms."

What? How? Why?

 Sooner or later every child will get to wondering, and ask the questions, "Where did I come from or how was I born? Am I really the child of my parents or was I adopted? Do I really belong to them?" The child of God will have questions also.

What Happened?

You have met a Person. Salvation is not something, it is *Somebody*. You received Jesus as your Saviour, and He gave you *His life* and *His nature*. Salvation is the miracle of receiving life, *Christ's life* (I John 5:11).

God does not promise your conversion will be emotional, although it may be. He does not promise it will be spectacular, as the apostle Paul's or sensational. But in Revelation 3:20 He does say if you open the door He *will come in*. Feelings change like the weather, but His Word "liveth and abideth forever" (I Peter 1:23).

Faith is just taking God at His word to keep His promises. *You are held by a threefold cord:*

1. Perfection of Christ's redemption (Hebrews 9:12).
2. Promise of Christ's word (John 6:40).
3. Purpose of Christ's will (John 17:24).

New Testament Reading Record

Each day as you finish reading, draw a line through the number of each chapter you have read that day. For example, suppose the first day you read 3 chapters in John, the next day 5 more, the next day 3, etc.

John	~~1 2 3 4 5 6 7 8 9 10 11~~ 12 13 14
John	1 2 3 4 5 6 7 8 9 10 11 12 13 14 15 16 17 18 19 20 21
I Peter	1 2 3 4 5
II Peter	1 2 3
Galatians	1 2 3 4 5 6
Ephesians	1 2 3 4 5 6
Mark	1 2 3 4 5 6 7 8 9 10 11 12 13 14 15 16
I Corinthians	1 2 3 4 5 6 7 8 9 10 11 12 13 14 15 16
II Corinthians	1 2 3 4 5 6 7 8 9 10 11 12 13
I John	1 2 3 4 5
II John	1
III John	1
Jude	1
Luke	1 2 3 4 5 6 7 8 9 10 11 12 13 14 15 16 17 18 19 20 21 22 23 24
Acts	1 2 3 4 5 6 7 8 9 10 11 12 13 14 15 16 17 18 19 20 21 22 23 24 25 26 27 28
I Thessalonians	1 2 3 4 5
II Thessalonians	1 2 3
I Timothy	1 2 3 4 5 6
II Timothy	1 2 3 4
Titus	1 2 3
Philemon	1
Philippians	1 2 3 4
Colossians	1 2 3 4
Romans	1 2 3 4 5 6 7 8 9 10 11 12 13 14 15 16
Hebrews	1 2 3 4 5 6 7 8 9 10 11 12 13
James	1 2 3 4 5

Matthew	1 2 3 4 5 6 7 8 9 10 11 12 13 **14**
	15 16 17 18 19 20 21 22 23 24 25 **26**
	27 28
Revelation	1 2 3 4 5 6 7 8 9 10 11 12 13 14
	15 16 17 18 19 20 21 22

Date started reading New Testament ....

Finished ....

If you read 3 chapters daily, you will finish in 87 days. The New Testament may be read in many ways. You may read it through consecutively, or in the order which we suggest above. Do not forget to mark what you read even if it is only a chapter.

MEMORY HELPS

Most people have difficulty when they start to memorize Scripture. This is like any other ability; it takes practice. You do not become a doctor, or a football star, or anything else without practice and work.

The more you memorize the easier it becomes. It does not take time to memorize; it actually saves time. You can use minutes all day long that would otherwise be wasted. People who think they are so busy they can't find time for any other type of Bible study can memorize.

In order to think your way through different verses, these illustrations are used for association and application.

Take some little cards and type or print your memory verses with references. Use one card for each verse. Most verses will fit on a 2×3-inch card. Writing the verse will help you remember it. The extra blessings are for those who want to go all the way with God.

SHOTS *for Protection Against the Disease of—*

1. Doubt of salvation (I John 5:11, 12).
2. Doubt of victory in temptation (I Corinthians 10:13).
3. Doubt of forgiveness (I John 1:9).
4. Doubt of provision and care (John 16:24).

QUESTIONS

1. You have met the Lord Jesus Christ and received Him as your personal Saviour, and He gave you (John 14:6; Gal. 2:20; I John 5:11) — *Check the correct or most nearly correct answer.*

   ☐ (a) a new chance
   ☐ (b) His life
   ☐ (c) new rules

2. John 3:18 says in the past you were _____

3. John 10:28 says you now have _____

4. "Eternal" means _____

5. John 5:24 says the Christian may some day be condemned for his sins.   T   F   ☐ ☐

6. God wants you to know if you have eternal life (I John 5:13).   T   F   ☐ ☐

7. Jesus says in John 6:37 that those who are not too wicked can come to Him.   T   F   ☐ ☐

8. Jesus said His sheep would never perish (John 10:28).   T   F   ☐ ☐

9. No trouble, or care, or anything else can separate you from the love of Christ (Rom. 8:35-39).   T   F   ☐ ☐

10. You can be plucked from Christ's hand (John 10:28).   Yes No   ☐ ☐

11. Can you slip through Christ's finger when you are a part of that finger? (Body, flesh and bones: I Cor. 12:13; Eph. 5:30)   Yes No   ☐ ☐

12. God is willing to let some believers be lost (John 6:39).   T   F   ☐ ☐

13. Who stands behind Jesus as a double guarantee (John 10:29)? _____

14. Upon whose power does our salvation depend (I Peter 1:5)? _____

15. The Holy Spirit guides and keeps the Christian in this life. How long is He to be with the Christian (John 14:16, 17)? _____

16. John 14:16, 17 also says, "for he dwelleth *with* you, and shall be _____ "

17. You can depend on God's promises because He never lies (Num. 23:19).   T   F   ☐ ☐

18. Romans 10:17 teaches assurance of eternal life should depend upon
    - ☐ (a) your feelings
    - ☐ (b) your promise to reform
    - ☐ (c) the Word of God
    - ☐ (d) your good works
    - ☐ (e) church membership

19. If you do not believe the record, what do you make God (I John 5:10)? _____

20. Jesus does not expect your life to be different now that you are a Christian (John 8:11; II Co. 5:17).   T☐ F☐

21. A real believer should have peace and joy (John 14:27; 15:11).   T☐ F☐

22. John 8:31 teaches if you are His disciples you will continue in His _____

23. What means has God chosen to change your life (John 15:3)? _____

24. Where should you carry it (Ps. 119:11)?

_____

25. How can you show your love to Christ (John 14:21)? _____

26. Jesus said in John 13:34, 35 that all men would be able to tell you are His disciple if you keep this new commandment to
 ☐ tithe our money
 ☐ go to church on Sunday
 ☐ love one another

27. Only preachers and Sunday school teachers are to spread the Gospel (John 20:21)   T☐ F☐

Have you memorized I John 5:11, 12 _____; I Cor. 10:13 _____; I John 1:9 _____; John 16:24? _____

LESSON 3

LEARNING TO EAT

A Battle Rages—

"For the good that I would I do not: but the evil which I would not, that I do" (Romans 7: 19). "For to will is present with me; but how to form that which is good I find not" (Romans 7: 18).

Many new Christians are surprised they have difficulty living the right kind of life. Their intentions are good. They try hard. Why do they usually fail?

A pig likes to eat garbage and lie in a mudhole; that is his nature. He is a pig. He does these things instinctively. A lamb likes to feed in green pastures and drink from clear, still water; that is the nature of a lamb.

If it were possible to take the nature of a lamb and place it in a pig, you would expect the pig to act like a lamb and feed in green pastures. He would still have the same body and look like a pig, but he would not act like a pig or enjoy the things the other pigs enjoy.

This illustrates what happened to you. You met the Lord Jesus and received Him as your personal Saviour. You were a sinner, but He has given you His life and His nature. You soon discover you have new interests. You want to do things you did not like to do before. This is the way it should be (II Peter 1:4).

Now suppose you find the pig has the new nature of a lamb, and he still has his old pig nature too. The chances are he will spend most of his time in the mudhole or eating garbage, because that is what he is in the habit of doing. Deep down in his heart, however, a battle will be raging. The nature of the lamb will be despising the filth and crying out for deliverance. The pig can never be happy in a mudhole again.

This is exactly the case with the new Christian. The old human, sinful nature is called the flesh. "That which is born of the flesh is flesh; and that which is born of the Spirit is spirit" (John 3:6). You have the fruit of the flesh and the Spirit contrasted in Galatians 5:19-23.

FOOD

The pig needs food. If he feeds in the pastures, we can expect him to act like a lamb. If he feeds on the garbage, we can expect him to act like a pig.

HOW CAN YOU GET HIM TO THE PASTURES?

If you could have someone to shepherd or

 guide the new pig it would help. Even so a pig is a hard animal to guide. He is headstrong and unpredictable. If you could put a guide right inside the pig's heart, what a difference that would make!

Jesus promised this very thing in John 14: 16, 17. The Holy Spirit is dwelling in the heart of every Christian. He is to be "with you" and "in you" forever (Romans 8:9; I Corinthians 6:19).

It is through the power of the Holy Spirit you are able to live the Christian life. In your own strength you can do nothing (Romans 7: 18). The rule for every Christian should be Galatians 5:16: "Walk in the Spirit [his power and guidance], and ye shall not fulfill the lust [strong desires] of the flesh."

Old habits will be very strong. This is a battle that will continue as long as you are in this body. Christ has promised you the victory if you will fight in His power and strength (Philippians 4:13; I Corinthians 15:57).

To grow spiritually you must have food. You must let the Holy Spirit guide you into the green pastures of God's Word. This should become a regular habit, not haphazard sampling.

"Thy words were found, and I did eat them; and thy word was unto me the joy and rejoicing of mine heart: for I am called by thy name, O Lord God of hosts" (Jeremiah 15:16).

Parents are always happy when a child begins to feed himself. He may need a lot of help, and he cannot eat every kind of food, but this is a sign he is growing. What a tragedy if someone had to feed him the rest of his life! Many Christians are in this very condition. Their growth has been stunted (Hebrews 5:11-14).

Several different utensils are used in eating. Each one has its particular use, but all are for the one purpose of helping you get food into your body. You do not eat just because you like the taste of food. You know your body must have food for energy and growth. So you will use several different methods in feeding on the Word to grow spiritually.

HEARING

"Faith cometh by hearing, and hearing by the word of God" (Romans 10:17). You are now a part of the Body of Christ (I Corinthians 12: 13). He has given the Body (the Church) evangelists, pastors and teachers to build it up and equip it for service (Ephesians 4:11-16). This is God's desire, that you meet with other Christians. There is a place in your heart that can only be filled by fellowship with God's people (Hebrews 10:25).

You can *hear* the Word of God preached and taught several ways—

1. By attending a Bible-believing church, not only on Sunday but also during the week.
2. Through radio and TV broadcasts.
3. Bible conferences, conventions and camps.

Share in the blessings of years of study and experience of the great servants of God.

Learn to take notes so you can keep and pass on the treasures you receive.

Through the printed page you can sit at the feet of the great men of God of past ages.

READING

"Give attendance to *reading* (I Timothy 4:13). You should have a Bible-reading plan that will take you from Genesis through Revelation. After you finish the New Testament, start in at Genesis and continue to read straight through the Bible. This will—

1. Help keep before you the whole plan of God.
2. Give you an opportunity to review forgotten material.

3. Bring to your attention new subjects for study.

4. Tie all parts of your "feeding on the Word" together. You will find the passage the pastor preached on, the verses you memorized, and the portion used in your study courses. So in this way you get the bird's-eye view of God's program.

You should eventually try to read through your Bible every year. You can do this by reading 3 chapters daily and 5 on Sunday. Keep this goal before you, but read to receive a blessing not for speed.

Children are trained to brush their teeth by using a health chart to mark every day. They are not expected to keep a chart the rest of their lives, but it is hoped a visible record will help them develop the habit of brushing their teeth.

Remember to mark your reading chart so you will develop the daily habit of "feeding on the Word."

Take time after reading for God to speak to you.

STUDYING

"*Study* to show thyself approved unto God, a workman that needeth not to be ashamed, *rightly* dividing the word of truth" (II Timothy 2:15; Acts 17:11). Many families try to make

Sunday dinner an especially good meal. It is important that at least once each week you really "dig down" into the Word and study. This should not be confused with reading. To prevent you from getting "bogged down" in your *reading* when you find an interesting subject, list it on a page in your notebook under the title, "Topics for Future Study." Otherwise you might spend weeks in a few chapters. Then study the subjects after you have finished reading the book.

As you study, be systematic, preserve the fruit of your effort, make it "pass-on-able," make a personal application to your own life. For example: This is what God's Word says—but this is what I am doing—so I will seek to change my life in this way.

TYPES OF BIBLE STUDY

1. Question and answer (as you are now doing in this course).
2. By topics (prayer, temptation, love, Satan).
3. People in the Bible.
4. By book, chapter, verse or words.
5. Survey.

A list of suggested studies are given at the end of this course. It is important first to lay a good foundation, meet your present needs, and develop good study habits.

You may want to devote an evening to your weekly study or portions of several days. Try to work on at least one Bible study each week.

A knife is used to cut food. Learn to *rightly divide* the Word (II Timothy 2:15).

Are you looking up all the references given in this part of the lesson?

MEMORIZING

"Thy word have I hid in mine heart, that I might not sin against thee" (Psalm 119:11). In eating you use a fork to pick up bites of food. As you feed on God's Word you will find promises, commands, words of wisdom, or choice bites that you will want to remember. There are many reasons for hiding the Word in your heart where it will always be with you. It is automatic machinery that the Holy Spirit can use (John 14:26):

1. To meet the attacks of Satan (*you have the first four verses especially for this*)
2. To win another (I Peter 1:23).
3. To help you grow (Acts 20:32; I Peter 2:2, 3).
4. To change your life (Romans 12:2; II Corinthians 3:18; Hebrews 4:12).
5. To set a standard (Psalm 19:7, 8).
6. To pray more effectively (John 15:7; Colossians 1:9-11).
7. To guide you (Psalm 119:105).

Do what the Bible says: Hide the verse in your heart, not your head.

Spend the time necessary to learn the reference so you can always turn to it in your Bible and use it with someone else.

As you read and study you will find verses you would like to memorize. List them on a page in your notebook, "Verses for Future Memory." Learn the verses with the lessons first before you go "on your own." They are matched with the study section and are selected to give you a foundation and to meet your immediate needs.

The secret of memory work is review. In order to review you need some type of system. That is why the verse cards are used. Soon it will take more time for review than it will for studying new verses. Use odd moments, waiting for or riding the bus, washing dishes, ironing, walking to work. Try for a goal of 3 new verses a week. In 10 years you would have 1,560 verses the Holy Spirit can use in your life and the lives of others.

DIGESTING

"*Meditate* upon these things; give thyself wholly to them; that thy profiting may appear to all" (I Timothy 4:15).

All the food in the world will not help you grow if your body does not digest it. It will just make you uncomfortable or sick.

Regardless of how much you *hear, read, study or memorize* the Word, if you do not digest it spiritually so it can be applied to your life it will not help you. (You will not be able to start all of these things and do them the right way at first. Satan will try to keep you out of the Bible.)

In Hebrews 5:11-14 it speaks of some people who had never grown spiritually. They were still babes and needed to be taught. Those who "by reason of use" had grown were ready for the "strong meat," the deeper truths of God's Word.

Throughout this course as you discover God's will, you will be urged to take little steps and apply what you have learned to your own life. This will in turn allow you to walk in closer fellowship with Christ and partake of the *abundant life* He offers.

SUGGESTIONS AND HELPS

Mark your Bible. Anything that will make you more at home in your Bible ought to be encouraged. Underline precious passages, circle the numeral of each verse you memorize, write cross references in the margin, and add descriptive words or comments. *But* do it carefully and neatly.

A concordance is a book containing lists of all the words used in the Bible and the places where they occur. It is very helpful to find a verse when you remember only a part of it or only a word. It is a valuable book too in the study of topics.

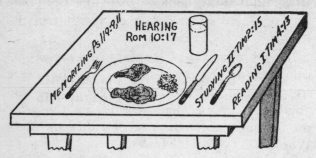

MEMORY HELPS

Hearing—Romans 10:17. The easiest way to feed upon the Word is by hearing it preached or taught.

Reading—I Timothy 4:13. The easiest way to feed yourself is by reading the Bible for yourself.

Studying—II Timothy 2:15. As you start reading the Word you will soon realize there are some things you will not be able to understand by just casual reading. You will have to stop and reread the portion and compare scripture with scripture. You will really have to study.

Memorizing—Psalm 119:11. As you really study you will come across verses you will want to remember. These you will want to memorize so you will always have them with you and the Holy Spirit can use them to encourage and guide you. As you hear the Word preached and taught, and you read and study and memorize for yourself, you will want to meditate on all these things and apply them to your life so the

Word of God can really change you into the image of Christ (II Corinthians 3:18).

Assignment:	Extra blessings:
Matthew 6:33	Jeremiah 15:16
Philippians 4:13	Romans 10:17
II Timothy 2:15	I Timothy 4:13
Psalm 119:11	I Timothy 4:15

QUESTIONS

1. Job 23:12 teaches that God's Word is more important than food.   T ☐ F ☐

2. II Tim. 3:16 teaches that all Scripture is inspired by God and is profitable for study.   T ☐ F ☐

3. Who helps you understand spiritual things (I Cor. 2:9-12)? _____
(The Author knows more about His Book than anyone else. You will not understand everything but you can claim God's promise in Deut. 29:29).

4. According to Ps. 119:18 you should begin to read the Bible by praying that God will
_____

5. The Bible will some day pass away (Isa. 40:8).   T ☐ F ☐

6. God still allows men to add to the Bible (Rev. 22:18).   T ☐ F ☐

7. Your unsaved friends can understand and appreciate spiritual things (I Cor. 2:14).   T ☐ F ☐

8. The Word of God is able to—
   (*Match the correct reference with the answer.*)

   ☐ Acts 20:32   (a) help you to pray
   (b) guide you
   ☐ John 15:7   (c) "build you up and
   give you an inherit-
   ☐ Ps. 119:105   ance"

                                          T F

9. II Tim. 2:15 commands you to pray. ☐ ☐

10. Ps. 119:11 teaches you should memorize
Scripture so others will know you are T F
a Christian. ☐ ☐

11. Mark 7:21-23 teaches that the source of T F
evil desires is the heart. ☐ ☐

12. You should learn to study because Eph.
4:14 teaches there are false teachers wait- T F
ing to deceive you. ☐ ☐

13. What verse in all the lessons has meant the
most to you (*not only the memory verses*)?
_____ Have you shared
it with anyone? _____

14. How many chapters have you read this week?
_____ Since starting the course? _____
(Speed is not the important thing but regular-
ity with an open heart.) Can you say *yes* to
Ps. 122:1? _____ How many services did
you attend last week? _____

15. What are four ways we can feed on God's Word? (*Match the correct answers and references.*)

- ☐ Hearing   (a) II Tim. 2:15
- ☐ Reading   (b) Rom. 10:17
- ☐ Studying   (c) Ps. 119:11
- ☐ Memorizing   (d) I Tim. 4:13

16. Most important you must apply the Word to your _____

17. By yourself you can do nothing for God T F (John 15:5).   ☐ ☐

18. Through whose strength should you live your daily life (Phil. 4:13)? _____

19. Whom did Andrew find after he had found Jesus (John 1:41)? _____

20. Have you ever led anyone to Christ? _____
Would you like to?   _____
Would Jesus like you to (John 15:16)? _____

21. To be used of God you

- ☐ I Cor. 1:26-29
- ☐ II Cor. 12:9
- ☐ Phil. 2:3, 4
- ☐ Col. 3:1, 2

(a) should not set your affections on earthly things.
(b) do not need to be wise, strong or important
(c) must work humbly
(d) work in Christ's power

Have you memorized Matt. 6:33 _____;
Phil. 4:13 _____; II Tim. 2:15 _____;
Ps. 119:11? _____

If you want an extra blessing learn: Jer. 15:16 _____; Rom. 10:17 _____; I Tim. 4:13 _____; I Tim. 4:15 _____

LEARNING TO TALK

SONS AND HEIRS—IN THE WEALTHIEST FAMILIES
IN THE UNIVERSE

"But as many as received him, to them gave he power to become the sons of God" (John 1:12). "Heirs . . . and joint-heirs with Christ" (Romans 8:14-17; I Peter 1:3, 4). What an amazing thing it is that God wants you to come to Him in prayer! He says: "Call unto me, and I will answer thee, and show thee great and mighty things, which thou knowest not" (Jeremiah 33:3). How hard it is to understand that God wants to do this for you! But God loved you so much that He gave you His Son, and with His Son He has promised to "also freely give us all things" (Romans 8:32).

When God created the universe He made certain natural laws by which the world runs. There are many of them and they cover every phase of activity—the law of gravitation; summer and winter; seed-time and harvest; the fruit tree yielding fruit after its kind; every winged fowl after its kind; whatever a man sows he shall also reap; and the soul that sins shall die.

But God often intervenes and changes things. The question arises, "If God knows all things, why should I pray about anything? He knows my needs better than I do." The answer is that prayer is God's chosen way for your obtaining and His changing things for you.

James 4:2 says: "Ye have not, because ye *ask* not." And Matthew 7:7, 11, "*Ask*, and it shall be given you; seek, and ye shall find; knock, and it shall be opened unto you. . . . If ye then, being evil, know how to give good gifts unto your children, how much more shall your Father which is in heaven give good things to them that *ask* him?"

We will study the privilege and power of prayer in several different ways.

1. As redeemed sons in the household of God (Galatians 4:4-7; Ephesians 2:19). You can come to God as your Father and expect Him to hear your requests because now you can come in Jesus' name (John 16:23, 24).

2. As communion with Him, that you "may know him" (Philippians 3:10; I John 1:3).

3. As ambassadors for Christ (II Corinthians 5:20). You are laborers in partnership with God.

The *privilege* of *prayer* can be compared to a bank account. It is just as though a millionaire had left you a book full of signed checks. Then to make sure they are honored he goes to the bank and identifies each check as it comes in. God knows all your needs and weaknesses. He would not honor any re quest that would injure or harm you or disgrace His name.

Jesus has left great and precious promises for you. He has ascended into Heaven and is now at the right hand of God making intercession for you (Hebrews 4:15, 16).

PRAYER CAN DO ANYTHING THAT GOD CAN DO

Banks require checks to be filled out in a certain way. God is able to do all things that are true to His nature and character. You cannot expect God to help you do something wrong because He cannot sin, and you could not ask that in the name of Jesus. This is the real test: Will it honor the name of Jesus?

"YE ASK, AND RECEIVE NOT,

Because ye ask amiss, that ye may consume it upon your lusts [selfish desires]" (James 4:3).

You must have the right attitude, but the scriptural way is still to ask.

Money in the bank cannot help unless your checks are cashed, *so ask!*

Prayer Releases the Energy of God

Faith

"And all things, whatsoever ye shall ask in prayer, believing, ye shall receive" (Matthew 21: 22).

Faith Is Expecting God to Act Like God

It is taking His promises to Him and expecting Him to answer. "Hear my prayer . . . in thy faithfulness answer me" (Psalm 143:1).

According to His Will

God reveals His will in His Word. The more you understand and know His Word the better you will be able to pray (I John 5:14, 15).

Prayer could be defined as talking with God. You could divide it into at least five different parts.

1. *Thanksgiving*—your appreciation for what He has done for you.
2. *Petition*—asking for things.
3. *Confession*—agreeing or saying the same thing about your sins as the Holy Spirit says, as He points them out to you.
4. *Intercession*—asking for others.
5. *Praise*—worship and reverence toward Him.

You have been studying about petitions; now look at the importance of thanksgiving. The Bible says:

1. "With thanksgiving let your requests be made known unto God" (Philippians 4:6).

2. "Pray without ceasing. In everything give thanks" (I Thessalonians 5:17, 18) .

THANKSGIVING

Every time you thank God you remember His goodness and the prayers He has answered for you in the past. This strengthens your faith and gives the assurance that He will also answer your other requests.

It is only common courtesy to thank someone who has helped you. Think how much you owe God! Jesus gave the example of giving thanks before meals (John 6:11) . This is something all can and should do.

If you are a parent you have a special responsibility. If you do not have prayer before meals, will you take the following step? Will you begin to give thanks before meals in your home today? _____

SUGGESTIONS FOR GOOD PRAYER HABITS

1. Do not constantly repeat the Lord's name.
2. Do not repeat the same old phrases.
3. Do not pray *at* others.
4. Do not pray *to* others.
5. Do not pray showy prayers to impress others.
6. Do not mumble or talk too softly in public prayer.
7. Do talk naturally, but reverently.
8. Do be definite; do not wander.
9. Do set aside a certain time for daily private prayer, a "quiet time" with God.

THE WORD
JOHN 15:7

PRAYER
JER. 32:27; 33:3

MEMORY HELPS

In order to pray effectively as a child of God, you need to learn the privileges, promises and restrictions as revealed in God's Word. It is important that you keep a balance in your life between prayer and Bible study.

Prayer without Bible study leads to fanaticism. Bible study without prayer leads to coldness.

Assignment:

    Jeremiah 32:27; 33:3

    John 15:7

Extra Blessings:

    Matthew 21:22

    I John 5:14, 15

    Philippians 4:6, 7

    Romans 8:32

QUESTIONS

1. One of your first prayers should be, "Lord, teach us to pray" (Luke 11:1).   T ☐   F ☐

2. Christians can now pray in the name of Jesus (John 16:24).   T ☐   F ☐

3. As you pray to God, your motive should
   be to bring glory to yourself (John   **T   F**
   14:13) .   ☐ ☐

4. Ephesians 2:18 teaches that we normally pray
   to the Father through _____
                   by the _____

5. Some of the requirements for effective prayer
   are—

☐ Matt. 21:22	(a) abide in Christ
☐ I John 5:14, 15	(b) believe
☐ John 15:7	(c) ask according to His will
☐ John 15:7	(d) His Word abide in us
☐ I John 3:22	(e) not ask selfishly
☐ James 4:3	(f) live obediently

6. What sometimes hinders our prayers (Isa. 59:
   1, 2) ? _____

7. If you sin how do you get back on praying
   ground (Ps. 32:5) ? _____

8. Some of the times you should pray are—

☐ I Thess. 5:17	(a) when tempted
☐ Heb. 4:16	(b) when afflicted
☐ Matt. 26:41	(c) without ceasing
☐ James 5:13	(d) evening, morning and noon
☐ Ps. 55:17	(e) in times of need

9. Some of the people for whom you should pray are—

☐ Eph. 6:18	(a) your enemies
☐ Matt. 5:44	(b) all saints (Christians)
☐ James 5:14-16	(c) all men, kings, those in authority
☐ I Tim. 2:1, 2	(d) the sick
☐ I Tim. 2:4	(e) the unsaved

10. Some of the things you should pray for are—

☐ James 1:5	(a) strength
☐ Acts 4:29	(b) that the Lord will teach you
☐ Ps. 19:12	(c) boldness to witness
☐ Ps. 105:4	(d) wisdom
☐ Ps. 119:33	(e) cleanse me from secret faults
☐ I Peter 5:7	(f) a knowledge of His will for you
☐ Col. 1:9	(g) all your cares

11. Prayers were offered from the following physical positions in the Bible:

☐ Mark 11:25	(a) on His face
☐ I Kings 19:4	(b) sitting
☐ Luke 22:41	(c) standing
☐ Matt. 26:39	(d) kneeling

12. Part of your prayer life should be what kind of prayer (Matt. 6:6)? _____

13. What should we avoid (Matt. 6:7)? ____ ____
_____

14. Who helps when you do not know how to express your thoughts or desires to God (Rom. 8:26, 27)? _____

15. Have you started a prayer list of unsaved friends? _____

How many chapters have you read the past week? _____ Have you memorized Jer. 32:27; 33:3 _____; John 15:7? _____

Extra blessings: Matt. 21:22 _____; I John 5:14, 15 _____; Phil. 4:6, 7 _____; Rom. 8:32? _____

LESSON 5

STARTING TO WALK

THREE CLASSES OF MEN

Once there was a wealthy family in which there were two sons. The father loved his sons and wanted the very best for them. So he hired a special teacher to train and teach and take care of his children. The father had particular jobs for which he wanted his sons trained.

Next door lived a neighbor boy who often played with the sons, but the teacher never tried to instruct him because he had not been hired to do that. The neighbor boy did not want to learn anyway and considered the things being taught as a lot of foolishness. The less time the

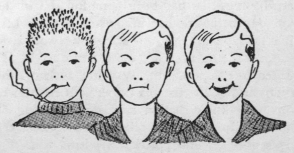

sons spent playing with the neighbor boy the more they seemed to learn.

In this family there was a difference in the attitude of the two sons. The one son, named *carnal*, never did like the teacher. He wanted to do things his own way, and was not interested in the lessons which the teacher had been asked to teach. He was always fighting and getting into trouble. He envied the other boys. He was always joining "gangs" and seemed to enjoy the neighbor boy's company more than his own family.

About all the teacher could do was to try to keep him out of trouble. The only time he seemed to listen was when he was in a "jam" of some kind and he needed help. *Carnal* never thought of anyone but him*self*. So, as soon as he was out of trouble, off he would go to find something to amuse himself.

The other son's name was *Spiritual*. He loved his father very much and wanted to please him. He realized that his father had an important position for him and remembered all the wonderful things that had been done for him in the past. He believed that his father had his best interests at heart, so he decided he would do whatever the new teacher wanted him to do. He wanted to co-operate in every way to learn the lessons and skills that his father wanted him to know. He knew that in this way he would be able to help his father sooner and assume the responsibilities and position awaiting him.

Spiritual was not a perfect child. He sometimes had to be reproved and corrected, but he had the right attitude and wanted to do what was right.

God Sees Three Classes of Men

Read I Corinthians 2:9—3:4.

The Natural man will compare with the neighbor boy. He is the unsaved man spoken of in I Corinthians 2:14. Spiritual things are foolishness to him. The Holy Spirit does not try to teach him about the wonderful things that God has prepared for them that love Him (verse 9).

The Second and Third Classes of Men Are Composed of Christians

The Carnal man will compare with the rebellious, head-strong son. He is spoken of in I Corinthians 3:1-4. "Carnal" means *fleshly*. It refers to someone who is trying to live the Christian life in his own strength.

Verse 1 calls him a "babe" in Christ; he has not grown as he should.

Verse 2 says he cannot be taught much.

Verse 3 says he is yet carnal and walks as men (in his own strength).

Verse 4 speaks of envy, strife and divisions among them; troublemakers.

THE SECOND CHRISTIAN

The spiritual man will compare with the obedient son who wants to do his father's will. He is spoken of in I Corinthians 2:15; 3:1. He sees and understands the things that are freely given to him of God. He is yielded to the Holy Spirit's guidance, and the fruit of the Spirit will be seen in his life (Galatians 5:22, 23).

THE WALK OF THE CHRISTIAN

The Christian's life may be illustrated by a father who sends his son for a walk. Now consider an obedient child who wants to obey his father.

No human father would send out his little son by himself, and neither has our heavenly Father. Jesus said just before he returned to Heaven: "I will pray the Father, and he shall give you another Comforter, that he may abide with you forever" (John 14:16).

The words "another Comforter" in the original language are full of meaning. "Another" could be translated "another just like me, of the same sort, with the same characteristics (as Jesus)." Comforter, from the Greek word paraclete, means "one called alongside to help." So literally Jesus said: "God will send you Another who will be just like Me and He will be alongside of you to help you forever." Then He goes on in the next verse to promise that the Holy Spirit would not only be with you but *in* you. The Holy Spirit plays an important part in the life of a *spiritual Christian*. But just because He dwells in all Christians does not mean that all are filled by the Spirit (Romans 8:9).

God's Desire—

"Be filled with the Spirit" (Ephesians 5:18). The tense of the verb in Greek would allow this translation, "Be constantly filled [controlled] by the Spirit." Many Christians never take advantage of this opportunity or *obey* this command. They try to walk in their own strength and wisdom. The happy life is the *Spirit-filled life*.

How May I Be Filled?

"In the last day, that great day of the feast, Jesus stood and cried, saying, If any man thirst let him come unto me, and drink. He that believeth on me, as the scripture hath said, out of his belly shall flow rivers of living water. (But this spake he of the Spirit)" (John 7:37, 39).

1. *Thirst* for—

The Holy Spirit to lead and teach you (John 16:13, 14).

The power of the Holy Spirit in your life (II Timothy 1:7).

The Holy Spirit to make you Christlike (II Corinthians 3:18).

The Holy Spirit to reproduce His fruit in your life (Galatians 5:22, 23).

The awareness of Christ's presence in your life (Ephesians 3:17-19).

Victory over temptation (I Corinthians 15: 57).

2. *"Come . . . and drink"*

This is the act by which the believer claims this promise for his own. He recognizes that he is not able to live his own life in a way that will be pleasing to God.

In II Corinthians 8:5 some people "gave their own selves to the Lord."

In Romans 6:13 we are told, "Yield yourselves unto God."

In Romans 12:1 we are told, "Present your bodies."

Presenting yourself to God is a definite final act (aorist tense in Greek). It need never be repeated. Presenting yourself to God is just agreeing that "ye are not your own" (I Corinthians 6:19, 20), and giving Him possession to what is rightfully His.

This *initial act* should be followed by a *continuous attitude*. Anything else is rebellion and will call for *discipline*.

PRESENT YOUR WHOLE SELF

This does not mean just giving Him the part of your life which is hard to manage and keeping the part you want. That would be like the man who took the hands of a clock to the jeweler because they were not keeping good time.

3. "Believeth on Me"

Whoever *thirsts* is to *come and drink* and *trust* in Him as the One who fills with His Spirit. Just as you believed in Jesus as your Saviour, now you are to believe that He will do what He says and fill or control you with His Spirit. A Christian's blessings are all obtained by faith (James 1:6).

Have you yielded yourself to Christ? He wants your entire body, soul and spirit to use to reveal Himself to others. *Will you do it now?* _____
Date _____

QUESTIONS

What will happen to me if I do not yield myself to God?

You will remain an unhappy spiritual "babe," a carnal Christian (as described in I Corinthians 3:1-4), able only to understand the "milk of the word." You will be like the seed that fell among thorns in the Parable of the Sower (Mark 4:19) : "And the cares of this world, and the deceitfulness of riches, and the lusts of other things entering in, choke the word, and it becomes unfruitful." Your choice, Do I want to be a carnal or a spiritual Christian?

Will God force me to yield my life to His control and be filled with the Holy Spirit?

No, this is voluntary. You personally accepted Jesus as your Saviour and received eternal life. Now you must personally decide if you want to be filled with the Holy Spirit and enjoy the abundant life Christ promised.

Do I have to be filled only once, and is that all that is necessary?

Being filled (controlled) by the Spirit is a moment by moment ministry of the Holy Spirit, but it must have a *beginning*. That is why you are told to "present your bodies" to God. You remain filled by being obedient to the Spirit's commands. Broken fellowship is restored by confesisng that disobedience to God (I John 1:9) .

Why must I depend upon the Holy Spirit?

It is through His ministry that you grow spiritually. God has a will and a plan for every life. But it is only through the guidance and teaching of the Holy Spirit that you can find, follow and fulfill this plan.

Think how unhappy a human father would be if he knew his new-born child would never grow up; would never be able to walk but would always have to be carried; would never be able to feed himself but would always have to be fed by someone else; would never be able to work with and help his father; would never be able to understand his father's words or talk to him.

This is exactly what happens to an unyielded Christian. He never learns to walk with God, to feed upon and understand God's Word, to be a co-laborer with God, or to pray to God. The sad thing is that it is his own choice because of unyieldedness.

How do I know that God will not ask me to do some hard thing, like becoming a missionary to some far country?

If He does, it will be the best thing you could possibly do. God will never ask you to do anything for Him without giving you power and wisdom to do the task.

How may I know if I am filled by the Spirit? Will there be an emotional experience?

Very likely, especially the first time you surrender your life to His control. Feelings vary, but everyone is affected by emotions at important occasions in their lives, such as engagements, weddings, graduations, or when saved. But everyone is not affected the same way. So do not look for or try to copy someone else's experience. The real sign that you are filled with the Spirit is when the fruit of the Spirit is seen in your life—love, joy, peace, longsuffering, gentleness, goodness, faith, meekness and self-control (Galatians 5:22, 23).

Must I know the exact time that I yielded myself to God?

No, many people probably do not know the exact time. But the important thing is to be certain you have done so. Then you will be able to meet the doubts that Satan will bring up to confuse you.

Must yielding my life to God take place at a later date, after I have been saved?

Many people undoubtedly yield themselves to God at the time they are saved. The important thing is not the time but that you *have* taken this step, so you may be filled with the Holy Spirit. Be sure; don't deceive yourself and miss the full, happy *abundant life* Jesus promised.

The Spirit-Filled Walk

First, consider an obedient son. As he and his teacher start out for a walk, probably the boy will not stay too close to the teacher even though he intends to do so. He may become interested in something exciting and become impatient and run ahead. The wise teacher does not try to teach everything at once but patiently takes one thing at a time. He knows just what to teach and when to teach it. Each child is different; so each is treated differently to meet his particular need and to train him to be fitted for his field or position in life.

Everyone is not a carpenter, nor a farmer, nor a doctor. The training is different for each one of these occupations. Some jobs require much more training and preparation than others.

 Suppose the father wants the teacher to train his son to fill a certain job in the family business. He gives the teacher some books and brochures, telling all about the assets, the organization, the policies, the plan of operation and the goals. As soon as the teacher reveals a rule or a program to the son, he must accept and abide by it or the teaching progress has stopped. Often the relationship between the pupil and teacher will become very unhappy. The son may even feel the father is unreasonable in his demands or old-fashioned in his ways.

As you walk along with the Holy Spirit, balanced upon the two legs of *prayer* and the *Word,* He will lead you down a path named, "the will of God." He will begin to point out things in the Word to you. There may be things you do not want to do, so you "hang back"; or things you want to skip so you can run ahead. The pattern will probably be a little different for you than anyone else. Satan will not have forgotten you and will try to tempt you away from a close walk of fellowship.

Obedience Is the Key to Fellowship

As the Holy Spirit reveals through the Word what God would have you do, you must accept it. If you are not obedient to it, you have stopped your progress and spiritual growth and fellowship is broken. Jesus said: "If ye keep my commandments, ye shall abide in my love" (John 15:10) ; and "If ye know these things, happy are ye if you do them" (John 13:17). So *obedience* is the key to *fellowship* and it *opens the door to happiness.*

The call to obedience is really a call to the heart or will. This is the thought of Ephesians 6:6: "Doing the will of God from the heart." This is the language of Christ when He said: "Not my will but thine be done." The *ability* and *strength* to follow and do the things God would have you do must come from God. Do not get side-tracked into legalism and think you must obey and perform these things either to add to your salvation or to make it better. "Are you so foolish? having begun in the Spirit, are ye now made perfect by the flesh?" (Galatians 3:3). (Your own ability.)

What happens if you say no to the Holy Spirit and disobey Him?

You break one of the two conditions for remaining filled with the Spirit. I Thessalonians 5:19 says, "Quench not the Spirit." (Quench

means to hinder, or to make ineffective. See how
it is used in Ephesians 6:16 and Hebrews 11:34.)
You quench (or make ineffective) His ministry
when you say *no* to Him and disobey His leading. Your fellowship is broken; you have placed
an obstacle between yourself and God.

"Grieve not the Holy Spirit of God" (Ephesians
    4:30).

Satan is constantly trying to tempt the Christian to sin. When you say *yes* to Satan and sin
you *grieve* the Holy Spirit. In these two ways
your fellowship can be broken so that you are
no longer controlled by the Spirit. When you
say—

1. *No* to the Holy Spirit and disobey Him
    (I Thessalonians 5:19).
2. *Yes* to Satan's temptation and sin (Ephe-
    sians 4:30).

Fellowship is restored by use of I John 1:9. Remember fellowship is the state of family relations. You are a member of the household of
God. When you sin you are a disobedient son.
You became a son when you were saved (John
1:12, 13; Galatians 4:5).

GOD'S PROVISION FOR A SPIRIT-FILLED LIFE

"This I say then, Walk in the Spirit [his guidance and power], and ye shall not fulfill the lust
[desire] of the flesh" (Galatians 5:16).

The Spirit-filled life is not a stationary life.
It is not a jelly-fish type of effortless existence.

It is not a "let-go-and-let-God" affair but a "take-hold-with-God" business. In order to grow, the Christian must exercise his free will, make choices, decide between right and wrong, say *no* to temptation and constantly try to improve his spiritual life and become more Christlike. But your calling is beyond your ability. It is like an engineer trying to push his train. His intentions are good, but he is not strong enough. However, as soon as he climbs into the cab and pulls the throttle the train starts moving down the track.

II Peter 1:5-7 says: "And beside this, giving all diligence, add to your faith *virtue;* and to your virtue *knowledge;* And to knowledge *temperance;* and to temperance, *patience;* and to patience *godliness;* And to godliness *brotherly kindness;* and to brotherly kindness *charity.*" There is a similar passage in Philippians 4:8.

To do these things in your own strength is like trying to push the train. But the instant you say *yes* to the Spirit's leading and move in that direction He is there with His wonderful energizing power. It is just like pulling the throttle on the train.

Whatever God asks you to do, He will give you the power to do it.

The Spirit-filled life is a life of constant *growth*. If you are not growing you are sick spiritually. It is the only way to overcome the evil desires of the flesh (old nature) (Galatians 5:16).

MEMORY HELPS

Ephesians 5:18 commands you to be filled (controlled) by the Holy Spirit. If you really want to do this, if you thirst for the power of the Spirit in your life, and come to Christ, and believe and trust that He will fill and control your life by His Holy Spirit, then you are able to walk in the Spirit-filled life through the power of the Holy Spirit as promised in Galatians 5:16. As long as your life remains yielded to Him, you can continue this walk. There are

two detours that might take you from it—if you say *no* to the Holy Spirit as He seeks to guide you, or if you say *yes* to some temptation of Satan as he seeks to lure you away.

Assignment:

Romans 6:13
Ephesians 5:18
John 15:10

Extra blessings:

John 7:37-39
I Thessalonians 5:19
Ephesians 4:30
John 13:17
I Corinthians 2:12

QUESTIONS

1. John 16:13, 14 teaches that the Holy Spirit will not speak of Christ but will glorify Himself.   T F   □ □

2. The Holy Spirit is called—

   □ John 14:16   (a) Spirit of God, Spirit of Christ
   □ John 14:17   (b) eternal Spirit
   □ Heb. 10:29   (c) the Comforter
   □ Rom. 1:4   (d) Spirit of truth
   □ Rom. 8:2   (e) Spirit of grace
   □ Eph. 1:17   (f) Spirit of holiness
                   (g) Spirit of wisdom and revelation
   □ Heb. 9:14   (h) Spirit of power, love, and a sound mind
   □ Rom. 8:9
   □ II Tim. 1:7   (i) Spirit of life

3. All Christians have been—

   □ John 3:5, 6   (a) indwelled by the Holy Spirit
   □ Eph. 1:13   (b) baptized into the Body of Christ by the Holy Spirit
   □ I Cor. 12:13
                   (c) born of the Spirit
   □ I Cor. 6:19   (d) sealed by the Spirit
                   (e) comanded to be filled
   □ Eph. 5:18   by the Holy Spirit

4. There are three classes of men mentioned in I Cor. 2:14—3:4—

☐ Natural man

☐ Carnal man

☐ Spiritual man

(a) the unyielded Christian living in the power of his own flesh

(b) unsaved man

(c) the Christian living in the power and guidance of the Holy Spirit

6. List the three steps in the order Jesus gives in John 7:37-39, whereby you may be filled with the Spirit:

☐ First step

☐ Second step

☐ Third step

(a) come and drink.

(b) thirst.

(c) believe that God will fill you.

7. If you permit Him, the Holy Spirit will—

☐ Rom. 8:26, 27

☐ Rom. 5:5

☐ I Cor. 2:12

☐ I Cor. 2:13

☐ Rom. 8:16

☐ Eph. 3:16

☐ Rom. 8:14

(a) strengthen you

(b) lead you

(c) help you to pray

(d) teach you

(e) shed the love of God in your heart

(f) show you the things God has given you

(g) assure you that we are children of God

8. When the disciples were filled with the Holy Spirit they became very timid T F (Acts 4:31). ☐ ☐

9. To remain filled with the Holy Spirit you must not _____ or _____ Him (Eph. 4:30; I Thess. 5:19).

10. What is the key to fellowship (John 15:10)?
_____

11. If you sin and fellowship is broken, how can you get back into fellowship (I John 1:9)?
☐ do penance
☐ be rebaptized
☐ confess your sin to God

12. Jesus was not empowered by the Holy
Spirit (Luke 3:21; Acts 10:38). T F ☐ ☐

13. If it was necessary for Him, will it be necessary for you (Rom. 7:18; Eph. 5:18)? _____

14. Romans 12:1 says for you to—
☐ do the best you can.
☐ keep the Ten Commandments.
☐ present yourself to God.

15. Do you think He wants to make you happy or miserable? _____
Do you think He is wiser than you are (Ps. 18:30)? _____
Do you think He will take advantage of you and *make* you do things you do not want to do (I John 5:3)? _____
You have made Christ your Saviour, but have you made Him the Lord of your life? If not, will you do so now? *(Make a note of the date in the flyleaf of your Bible so you won't forget. God will remember.)*

How many chapters have you read this past week?
_____ Hiding verses in your heart will pay big dividends. It is very important. Do not try to memorize too fast. Take two or three verses a week and review your old verses.

Have you memorized Eph. 5:18 _____;
Rom. 6:13 _____; John 15:10? _____

Extra blessings: John 13:17 _____; John 7:37-39
_____; I Cor. 2:12 _____; Eph. 4:30 _____;
I Thess. 5:19 _____

WALKING WITHOUT STUMBLING

TEMPTATION

Suppose the father asks his son, named *Spiritual*, to go to the store and buy a 50-cent can of paint. He gives him a five-dollar bill and says that 25 cents will be his to keep but to bring back the change.

He tells his son he can spend 25 cents for anything he likes except something to eat, because it is almost dinner time. He also instructs the teacher to go along.

The storekeeper is not very honest; he is only interested in getting people's money. He tries to make people think he is kind to them so he can trick them into spending more money.

There happens to be a "special" on paint and the storekeeper wants to sell the boy three cans for $1.00. He tries to convince him that his father will be very proud of him for taking advantage of

70

the bargain. *Spiritual* only buys one can, however, because his teacher reminds him that his father had said, "Buy one can of paint."

The storekeeper, eager to get more of the boy's money, suggests that he might like to visit the candy counter. *Spiritual* is getting very hungry, and he does have a quarter that belongs to him. But the teacher says, "Remember your father said not to get anything to eat." So the boy turns to the toy counter, eager to spend his 25 cents.

There were many toys he would like to buy. After a few helpful words from the teacher he selects a nice toy and is ready to return home.

The storekeeper is not going to give up so easily. He calls his own son to one side and tells him to help persuade *Spiritual* to spend more money.

The storekeeper's son comes and says, "Say, have you seen the new footballs Dad has? Why don't you get one? Your father is rich and he wouldn't care." *Spiritual* had been wanting a football all summer. The storekeeper, seeing he is interested, becomes almost insistent. This scares *Spiritual* and he is glad his father sent the teacher along. He steps a little closer to him, then tells the storekeeper, "No, my father said I should bring the change back to him!" The storekeeper quickly mutters an apology and does not try to sell him anything else, for he is afraid to make *Spiritual's* father angry.

As the boy passes the candy counter on the way out, he stops just to look. His stomach seems very empty and he knows if he stays any longer he will have to buy some. He turns to ask the teacher what to do, but he is at the door already, holding it open for him. *Spiritual* grabs his paint and runs out the door. On the way home he passes an apple tree loaded with beautiful red apples. He would like to steal one but a word from his teacher reminds him that it is wrong to do this.

Upon arriving at home, the boy delivers the paint and money to his father. Upon learning of his experiences, and the way he has resisted temptation, his father is proud of him and gives him a special reward.

Many Christians are surprised that they are still tempted after they are saved. But the Bible teaches that even spiritual leaders are to be careful so they will not be tempted and fall into sin (Galatians 6:1; I Corinthians 10:12). The wise thing to do is to *expect* temptation.

You have made Satan very angry when you became a Christian. Now he will redouble his efforts to make you sin and look bad before the world and ineffective in the service of Christ. Satan is represented in our story by the store-keeper. He tries to fool people just like the storekeeper and often appears as an "angel of light" (II Corinthians 11:14).

Temptation is as necessary to make strong Christians as exercise is necessary for an athlete.

It is harmless unless you give in to it. In fact, it will make you grow and able to meet stronger tests in the future.

How Will Satan Tempt Us?

 "Every man is tempted when he is drawn away of his own lust [desire] and enticed" (James 1:14).

Satan will tempt and try to lead you into sin through things you already desire. Remember the story of the pig and the lamb in Lesson 3? The Christian still has his old nature as well as his new nature. So one way will be through old sinful habits and desires. Perhaps Satan will send a friend and use him to tempt you. The Bible warns: "If sinners entice thee, consent thou not" (Proverbs 1:10). One of the best ways to avoid being tempted by old habits or desires is to "go not in the way of evil men" (Proverbs 4:14). Just stay away from people and places that might tempt you. "Make not provision for the flesh, to fulfill the lusts [desires] thereof" (Romans 13:14).

Good Desires

Satan also uses your good desires to lead you into sin. The storekeeper tried to use *Spiritual's*

desire to please his father to lead him into disobedience by buying three cans of paint instead
of one. He also tried to use the good desire for
food to tempt him.

Many times there will be both good and bad
desires mixed together in the temptation, such
as the desire to steal an apple and to eat it. Good
desires may be misused or there may be an over-
indulgence in them. Make a list (for your own
use) of the good and bad desires Satan might
use to tempt you.

How Can We Meet Temptation?

The teacher reminded
Spiritual of his father's
words. The Holy Spirit can
do the same for you by
using the Word of God.
This is the way Jesus met
temptation: "It is written—"
(Matthew 4:4). The Word
is the "sword of the Spirit" (Ephesians 6:17).
This is an important reason for hiding God's
Word in your heart (Psalm 119:11). If you have
it ready in your heart at all times, then the Holy
Spirit can use it to give you victory over temptation. When Satan tempts you do not argue;
quote a verse of Scripture.

Resist the Devil

Just as *Spiritual* had to take a stand and say
no to the storekeeper about the football, you will
also have to learn to say *no*. James 4:7 says:

"*Submit* yourselves therefore to God. *Resist* the devil, and he will flee from you."

FLEE THESE THINGS

There are other times when it is probably wiser to flee as *Spiritual* did. Look for that way of escape (I Corinthians 10:13; I Timothy 6:11).

SPECIAL TRAINING

The teacher provides special training for his student. He only matches him against tests for which he is ready.

The Holy Spirit will also guide so you can be victorious in temptation.

He assures you of four things—

1. That you will not face unusual tests such as other men do not have.
2. That God is faithful and will keep His promises.
3. That the tests will not be more than you are able to meet.
4. That if the test is more than a match for you, God will provide a way of escape (I Corinthians 10:13). This is an important verse. It promises you victory over temptation. Claim it!

TO THE PRAISE, HONOR AND GLORY OF CHRIST

How happy the father was that *Spiritual* had not fallen into sin! He was an honor to the family name. I Peter 1:6, 7 says that the trial of your faith is more precious than gold and should bring praise, honor and glory to Christ.

A CROWN

Spiritual was rewarded by his father. You shall also be rewarded.

"Blessed is the man that endureth temptation: for when he is tried, he shall receive the crown of life, which the Lord hath promised to them that love him" (James 1:12).

This is not salvation but a reward. Salvation is a gift (Ephesians 2:8, 9). You earn rewards.

MEMORY HELPS

Satan's Method	God's Faithfulness	For the Victorious
Your desires	No more than you are able to bear, or a way of escape	Rewards

| James 1:14 | I Corinthians 10:13 | James 1:12 |

The secret of memorizing is review. Go over
your verses every day until you have them "hidden in your heart." You can help your memory
by associating new things with old familiar
things. *Review! Review! Review! Review!
Review! Review! Review! Review! Review!*

Assignment: Extra blessings:
  James 1:14   Romans 13:14
  I Corinthians 10:13   I Peter 4:12
  James 1:12   Hebrews 2:18

QUESTIONS

1. There is no danger in trying to help
   someone who has fallen into sin because
   once we have reecived Christ we will be   T F
   free of temptation (Gal. 6:1).   ☐ ☐

2. A child of God can safely say he cannot   T F
   sin (I John 1:8, 10).   ☐ ☐

3. God sometimes tempts man to sin   T F
   (James 1:13).   ☐ ☐

4. Who is your chief enemy (I Peter 5:8)? ____
   _____

5. He is also called
   ☐ Matt. 4:3   (a) god of this world
   ☐ John 8:44   (b) tempter
   ☐ II Cor. 4:4   (c) Satan
                      (d) a liar
   ☐ Rom. 16:20   (e) appears as an angel
   ☐ II Cor. 11:14   of light

6. Satan has _____ (I Tim. 3:7) and
   _____ (II Cor. 2:11) to get Christians to sin.

7. You should _____ to God and _____
   the Devil (James 4:7). At times it may be
   wise to _____ from temptation (I Tim.
   6:11).

8. Jesus met temptation by quoting Scrip- T F
   ture (Matt. 4:6).   □ □

9. How can you prepare to follow His example
   (Ps. 119:11)? _____

10. According to Prov. 4:14; Eph. 4:27; and
    Rom. 13:14, you should not go to places
    or be with people whom the Devil can   T F
    use to tempt you to sin.   □ □

11. Satan will tempt you to do things you T F
    do not naturally like to do (James1:14). □ □

12. Sometimes a Christian is tempted by
    something greater than he is able to re-
    sist and he cannot help sinning (I Cor. T F
    10:13).   □ □

13. Christ is able to succor (help) you when
    you are tempted because He also was   T F
    tempted (Heb. 2:19; 4:15).   □ □

14. Who will give you victory over temptation
    (II Peter 2:9; I Cor. 15:57)? _____

15. Your victory over temptation and in testings
    will bring _____ and _____ and
    _____ to Christ at His appearing
    (I Peter 1:6, 7).

16. Will God reward those who are victorious in
    times of temptation (James 1:12)? _____

17. Temptation and sin mean the same   T F
    thing.   □ □

18. You are not only tempted to do evil but
    are sometimes tempted not to do good   **T   F**
    (James 4:17) .   □   □

19. Have you made a list (for your own use) of
    the good and bad desires Satan might use to
    tempt you? _____

20. Have you read Gen. 3; Job 1:7—2:10; Matt.
    4:1-17; James 1:1-16? _____

Do you have a systematic plan to commit Scripture
verses to memory? (Time, place, ways.) Have you
memorized James 1:14 _____; James 1:12?
_____

Extra blessings: Rom. 13:14 _____; I Peter
4:12 _____; Heb. 2:18 _____; Eph.
6:10, 11 _____; II Cor. 6:17, 18 _____

WASHING AND SPANKING

SIN!

To define sin, you could perhaps say "it is rebellion against God and His will." It is saying *yes* to Satan's suggestions and *no* to God's commands and exhortations.

The Christian becomes lax, does not heed the warning of the Holy Spirit, is tempted and falls into sin.

What happens now? Is he lost? Should he just forget his failure? What shall he do?

The penalty of sin is death. You were once under this condemnation (John 3:18; Romans 6:23). But "Christ hath redeemed us from the curse of the law, being made a curse for us" (Galatians 3:13). He paid the penalty for all your sins—past, present and future—and you have the promise that you "shall not come into condemnation [judgment]" (John 5:24). However, these new sins cannot be ignored.

If a son gets a traffic ticket for speeding and the father pays it, the legal obligation has been met. The court can never call him in again for this same offense, but this does not settle everything at home between the father and son. It is now a family problem. Fellowship has been broken. What must the son do to secure his father's forgiveness?

FELLOWSHIP—WHAT DOES IT MEAN?

The words translated fellowship and communion come from the same word in Greek. It means more than just friendship or comradeship. It means joint-participation or sharing of some common thing. It could be work, joy, sorrow, suffering, or many other things.

The key passage is I John 1:5—2:2. Read this portion before going on.

A FATHER AND SON

A father takes his small son for a walk. They enjoy walking together through a little park. They watch the birds flying, feed peanuts to the squirrels, and enjoy the beautiful flowers. In his eagerness to see and investigate all the wonders around him, the little son becomes quite dirty. As he comes to a stairway the steps look steep and dangerous to him. He sits down and goes down one step at a time. Of course he gets very dirty, but his father brushes him off. He does not mind because he knows his little boy does not know any better. But there are some things that cause a problem.

The father tells his son to stay out of the mud. The son thinks it will be fun to splash through it. Perhaps he sees other children playing in it. If he disobeys his father's commandment he also breaks the fellowship between them. They cannot enjoy this together.

THE KEY TO FORGIVENESS IS CONFESSION

Confession—The Greek word has an important meaning. It means "saying the same thing as another." Understanding this word is one of the most important things in understanding the Christian's life of fellowship.

Fellowship is immediately restored when the son says, "I was wrong getting into the mud." But if he says, "I haven't done anything wrong; the other children are playing in the mud," he is making his father a liar (I John 1:10).

The father will now be required to discipline the son so he can see his wrong and acknowledge it. Then the next time he is tempted he will not get into the mud.

GOD IS LIGHT

I John 1:5 tells us that "God is light." That is, according to His nature He is holy, sinless and pure. Verse 7 says: "But if we walk in the light, as he is in the light, we have fellowship one with another, and the blood of Jesus Christ his Son cleanseth us from all sin."

WASHING

If you obediently live in the light you possess, you will have fellowship with Him, just as the father and son in our story. While you do this, the blood of Jesus Christ cleanses (the Greek indicates constant action) from all sins of omission, sins of ignorance, sins you are unaware of, things you have not grown enough spiritually to recognize as sin. It is through this provision that sinful men can have fellowship with a holy God.

CONFESSION—AGREEING WITH ANOTHER

If the Holy Spirit through your conscience, a friend, or in some other way points out a certain thing you have done and says "that is sin," you are to confess or *agree* with Him, or say the same thing God says about it, and determine to put it out of your life and never do it again.

If you do this immediately, the only break in your fellowship will be during the act of sin, for God cannot participate with you in sin.

"He is faithful and just to forgive us our sins, and to cleanse us from all unrighteousness" (I John 1:9). Christ has already paid the penalty for your sins but God's purpose here is to cleanse from the defilement of sin, to make you more Christlike, to train and not to punish you.

If you refuse to *agree* with Him and to call

what you have done *sin*, as God has, then He will have to chasten (discipline) you.

Confession has to do with *known* sin, not *unknown* sin. It is sin that has become a distinct issue. As you grow spiritually, a few years from now you will see many things in your life which you do not recognize as sin today.

CHASTENING—SPANKING

Read Hebrews 12:5-13.

Chastening means disciplining, or correcting, or reproving. The word is used primarily in regard to child training. The object of chastening is training not punishment.

GOD'S THREEFOLD PURPOSE IN CHASTENING—

1. To cause you to acknowledge your sin so you may be restored to fellowship and be holy and without blemish (Ephesians 5: 27).

2. To reveal His Fatherhood and warn you that He deals with you as with a son (Hebrews 12:5-8).

3. To reward you. Sin may be the cause of loss of reward, not salvation (II John 1:8).

METHODS OF CHASTENING

A human father soon learns that he cannot train all his children in the same way. One child may be corrected by just talking to him; another may be totally different and require spanking; perhaps another must be denied some privilege. As a child grows the method of training him will probably change.

God is all-wise and will use the best method for each of his sons. You may be denied some privilege or have a favorite possession taken from you. God may send sickness, or a combination of these. All sickness should not be considered chastening, but it should call for soul searching (Psalm 139:23). Some children cannot be told but have to try everything for themselves, and God has the following method for them—

REAPING WHAT YOU SOW

Read Galatians 6:7-9.

God may let nature take its course. The unsaved also reap this type of judgment in both this life and the next. It often seems as though God hastens the harvest for the sinning Christian; that he reaps what he sows sooner than the unsaved. God uses reproach, suffering, or other consequences to chasten and bring him back to Himself.

ATTITUDES AND RESULTS OF CHASTENING

Despising—"Despite not thou the chastening of the Lord" (Hebrews 12:5). There are indications in the Scriptures that when Christians despise, hate or rebel against the Lord's chastening, He sometimes takes them Home. (See Proverbs 15:10; I Corinthians 5:5; 11:30; James 5:19, 20; I John 5:16.) This is a sobering thought. Children sometimes misbehave in public, and correction may not seem to do any good; rather than stay and bring reproach upon the family name the parents take the children home.

A Christian is made fit for Heaven by the shed blood and righteousness of Christ. But because of his conduct he might be unfit to continue to represent the household of God in this world.

Every premature death should not be regarded as a result of sin. On the other hand, be very careful not to despise God's chastening in your own life.

"Nor faint when thou art rebuked of him" (Hebrews 12:5). Do not be like the child who cries every time he is punished, because he is being disciplined and not because he regrets doing wrong. He gains no benefit from it.

GOOD RESULTS OF CHASTENING

It will bring forth "the peaceable fruit of righteousness unto them which are exercised thereby" (Hebrews 12:11).

It brings you back to the place where you will confess your sin, and be forgiven and cleansed (I John 1:9). In this way you become "partakers of his holiness" (Hebrews 12:10,).

How May You Escape Chastening?

"For if we would judge ourselves, we should not be judged. But when we are judged, we are chastened of the Lord, that we should not be condemned with the world" (I Corinthians 11:31, 32).

The Father is seen here waiting for the self-judgment or confession of His child. If the child will not judge the sin himself and confess that it is wrong, then the Father must judge it. God is longsuffering but He also loves you.

God shows His love to you by chastening even though at the time it may make you unhappy (Hebrews 12:6, 11). This is part of the method used to change you "into the same image [of Christ] from glory to glory" (II Corinthians 3:18).

Memory Helps

Purpose—Hebrews 12:11

Proper attitude of a son
Hebrews 12:5b

1. Not despising
2. Nor fainting

Chastening is by
the Father
Hebrews 12:7

The way to avoid chastening and self-judgment

I Corinthians 11:31, 32

then

I John 1:9
Psalm 32:5—Confessing

Assignment:
  Hebrews 12:5b
  Hebrews 12:11
  I Corinthians
    11:31, 32

Extra blessings:
  Hebrews 12:7
  Psalm 32:5

QUESTIONS

1. Match the following words and their meanings—

☐ Fellowship

☐ Confession

☐ Chastening

    (a) disciplining or training.

    (b) communion or joint-participation.

    (c) saying the same or agreeing with another

2. Becoming a Christian means that you **T F**
will not sin any more (I John 1:8, 10). ☐ ☐

3. If you deny this, what do you make God
(I John 1:10)? _____

4. Galatians 3:13 teaches your sins can be forgiven—
  ☐ if you promise to keep the law
  ☐ if you join the church, are baptized, and
    start to tithe
  ☐ because Christ redeemed you from the curse
    of the law

5. If a Christian confesses his sin, he is cleansed from the defilement of that sin and restored into fellowship with God (I John 1:9). T F ☐ ☐

6. After you have confessed your sin, you should not let Satan make you feel guilty by bringing it to your remembrance (Isa. 43:25). T F ☐ ☐

7. How many sins does God list in Proverbs 6:16-19 that He especially hates? _____

8. You can sin by not doing some good thing which you know you should do (James 4:17). T F ☐ ☐

9. Sin separates a Christian from God (Isa. 59:2). T F ☐ ☐

10. What might keep you from being restored into fellowship with God (Ps. 10:4)? _____

11. Psalm 139:23, 24 teaches you should try to hide your sins from God so He will not be offended. T F ☐ ☐

12. If you do not judge your sins God will chasten you (I Cor. 11:31, 32). T F ☐ ☐

13. You cannot prosper if you hide your sins (Prov. 28:13). T F ☐ ☐

14. If you are chastened you should—

☐ Rev. 3:19

☐ Heb. 12:11

☐ Heb. 12:5

(a) know God loves you
(b) not despise it nor faint because of it
(c) bring forth "the peaceable fruit of righteousness," if you have learned your lesson

Make a list *(for your own use)* of all the people you remember who have wronged you. Now go through the list one by one and forgive them (Eph. 4:32). Many Christians hinder their usefulness by an unforgiving spirit. Do not let this happen to you. Now destroy the list and do not let Satan use these incidents to bring bitterness into your life again.

Have you memorized Heb. 12:5b _____; Heb. 12:11 _____; I Cor. 11:31, 32? _____

Extra blessings: Heb. 12:7 _____; Eph. 1:7 _____; Ps. 32:5 _____; I John 1:7? _____

Have you read I John 1:5-2:2 _____; Heb. 12:5-13 _____; Gal. 6:7-9? _____ How many other chapters this week? _____

LESSON 8

ENJOYING THE FAMILY

GROWING THROUGH FELLOWSHIP WITH OTHERS

 Parents have found that in many ways it is easier to rear a family of several children than an "only child." With several children there is an added financial and material demand as well as the demand upon time, but it also has its advantages in the training of the children.

Children must have the opportunity to be around other children before they learn to share, to play, and to get along with others. After being around others, they soon enjoy sharing new discoveries, skills and knowledge. It is much more fun with someone their own age than an older person who already knows what they have just discovered. They enjoy teaching little brother something they have learned to do.

Parents are sometimes amazed at how easily the second child learns to do something it took the first one a long time to learn. The secret is

that the older child helped teach tne younger
or the younger imitated the older one. Children
profit from the experiences of each other. Sometimes a little girl will become a "little mother'
for the younger child. She will try to keep him
from getting hurt; show love and sympathy when
he gets hurt; or call Mother if help is needed.

The little brother is not only profiting from
her experience, but the little girl is learning lessons she will never forget.

The Christian Needs Fellowship

Private *reading, studying* and *memorizing* all
have their place in the life of the Christian. But
you need to meet with others and *hear* the Word
of God taught and preached, and share what
God has given others.

Like a Pebble in a Pond

You need to meet with
other Christians just as a
child needs to be around
other children. Your fel-
lowship should spread to
wider and wider circles
until it reaches the ends
of the earth.

In the last lesson you discovered that fellowship means more than just friendship. It means
joint-participation or sharing something in common with another.

Jesus chose only twelve from among all His
followers. But among the twelve there was an
inner circle of three—Peter, James and John.

It is important that you find someone of like precious faith, who is interested in the same things. You need someone with whom you can share the things you are discovering in God's Word. As problems arise your friend may be able to help because of his own experience or knowledge. You can be *prayer partners*. God gives a special promise to united prayer (Matthew 18:19).

Perhaps you do not know such a person. Pray about it. Ask God to send you someone. Usually someone about your own age and sex is best. However, God might send you someone quite a bit older (in age or in the Lord) to be a "spiritual" mother or father to you. Sometimes when you talk to a little child it is hard to understand what he is trying to say, so you ask his older brother or sister who can usually explain. Your prayer partner may be able to help you more than anyone else. Work out a fixed time, and plan to meet once a week.

THE HOME

In this first circle of fellowship should be your own family. There is nothing that will unite a family more and help it grow spiritually than fellowshiping together with Christ. This is sometimes called a family altar or family devotions. It is hard to lay down a strict pattern because each family is different. For a true fellowship of the family (joint-participation), it should not be so complicated that little children cannot understand most of it. It is unreasonable to think that a small child could benefit from hearing a chapter read from the Bible when he does not understand most of the words, any more than you would if it were read in a foreign language. A few verses explained will prove more valuable.

The method used should fit the needs of your family, whether it is reading a portion of the Bible, Bible or missionary stories, devotional guide, or Scripture verse promise box. Broadly speaking, it should include praise, thanksgiving (especially for answered prayer), feeding upon a portion of His Word, and all praying together. Will *you* start today? _____

DIFFICULTIES

All the members of your family may not know the Lord. It is especially difficult if the father is unsaved. You might have a family altar with only a part of your family present, while you pray for the salvation of the others. Work schedules may make it difficult for all to meet together. Set aside a certain time each day—at the breakfast table or in the evening. Make a time and keep it. *Don't* get too busy. *Family worship will pay big dividends.*

THE CHURCH

The next circle of fellowship should be the local church and the group of churches in its fellowship.

Every believer should become united with a local Bible-believing church. The local church provides many things the Christian needs, and fellowship that cannot be had in any other way. The Bible refers to the church in two ways:

1. As a local body of believers (Acts 8:1; 13:1; Philippians 4:15; Philemon 1:2).
2. As the Body of Christ composed of all believers around the world (I Corinthians 1:2; Ephesians 1:22, 23; 4:4; 12, 15, 16).

First, consider the local church and your relationship to it. Make it a matter of prayer as to the church you join. The name above the door will not always tell you what kind of a congregation meets inside the building.

Do Not Expect Perfection

No church is perfect. The pastor, the official board and the members are all human. They will make mistakes and so will you. With all its failures the church is the nearest approach to that perfect fellowship we will have some day in Heaven.

There Is a Difference

There is no question that some local churches are more like the church of the New Testament than others. Some have drifted so far from the Bible they are Christian in name only.

Do Not Pick a Church—

> because it has a beautiful building
> because of the preacher's personality
> because your friends go there
> because of family tradition

A YARDSTICK

Let us go to the Bible to see what a church should be like. God has given to the church pastors, evangelists and teachers (Ephesians 4:11, 12). A good pastor will gladly tell you what the church stands for and what he preaches and teaches.

1. Jeremiah 3:15 says a good pastor will feed his people with knowledge and understanding. I Peter 2:2 says you grow by the Word of God. "*All* scripture is given by inspiration of God" (II Timothy 3:16). *Do not* join a church that does not believe the Bible is the actual Word of God. (See II Timothy 3:1-7.)

2. Make sure the church upholds the deity of Christ, that He is God. "That Christ died for our sins . . . that he was buried, and that he rose again the third day according to the scriptures" (I Corinthians 15:3, 4). Some churches do not teach this (II Peter 2:1; I John 4:1, 2).

3. Do they have a midweek prayer meeting, and do they pray at this meeting? Is this where they take their problems and disagreements to settle them upon their knees?

4. Is the second coming of Christ taught (John 14:2, 3)? Some churches scoff at this (II Peter 3:3, 4).

5. Is there a constant effort made in soul winning? Are souls being saved? Are they conscious of the lost in their own community? Do they have a foreign missionary program? Are they supporting their own missionaries (Matthew 28:19, 20; Acts 1:8)?

You Will Not Find a Perfect Church

If the church is true to the Bible and faithful to the Gospel, even though there may be some flaws in conduct and practice, unite with it, contribute toward its spiritual advancement and you will grow with it.

Benefits for You

The program of a church could be divided into three main parts—

1. Teaching and training
2. Worship
3. Service

This is a large subject and we will consider only a few important points.

Teaching and Training of—

New members (sadly neglected in most churches) —II Timothy 2:2.

The children— (Proverbs 22:6; II Timothy 3:15).

Old members (for more effective service) — Ephesians 4:11-13.

WORSHIP

Jesus left two ordinances for the church—Baptism and the Lord's Supper. As you enter the church fellowship you will want to be obedient and be baptized (Matthew 28:19; Acts 10:48). It is an outward sign of an inward work of grace, the new birth. It speaks of identification with Christ in His death, burial and resurrection (Romans 6:4). Consequently, it should be for believers only. It could have no significance to anyone who does not believe or who cannot understand what it means.

Be present when the Lord's Supper is observed. "For as often as ye eat this bread, and drink this cup, ye do show the Lord's death till he come" (I Corinthians 11:26).

"GIVING" SHOULD BE A PART OF WORSHIP

There are expenses in operating a local church, and you should assume your part in this. The Jews in the Old Testament were commanded to give a tithe (one-tenth of their income) back to God. We are not commanded to do this today, but it is a good plan to start with. There is a much higher spiritual principle given in Proverbs 3:9, 10. Honor the Lord with your first-fruits. Do not wait until the whole harvest and then give the Lord His tithe. The promise is that if you take care of the Lord's work first you will have plenty. You should not get everything you want first and then give to God if you have anything left. As you survey the world, make a list of the different parts of God's work that require financial support. Pray for guidance that God will direct you to put His portion in the places where He would have you put it. *You should only give to causes that honor Christ.*

UNITED PRAYER

God gives a special promise to united prayer (Matthew 18:19). The midweek prayer meeting should be attended if at all possible. The members who are in business for God will usually be there. This is sometimes called "the hour of power." It is the "spiritual thermometer" of the church. If you are too timid to pray before other people participate silently. Ask God to teach you to pray (Luke 11:1).

SERVICE

Many activities are sponsored by the average church. Start praying that God will give you a place to serve Him. Speak to Him first about it. Be careful that you do not get involved in just "busy work."

The big task is to get the Gospel to the "uttermost part of the earth" (Acts 1:8). Everything else should have its relationship to that and "teaching them to observe all things whatsoever I have commanded you" (Matthew 28:20).

Learn to talk to people about Christ. Help support others who can spread the good news where you cannot go.

Do "good works." These are profitable (Titus 3:8). But use them as an opening to tell of God's unspeakable gift. This is the greatest thing you can do.

Too Big

The task of world evangelization is too big for one church, or group of churches.

One Body

The Church is also spoken of as the Body of Christ. He is the Head. All "born-again" Christians make up His Body, the Church (Ephesians 4:4; 5:23). Christ prayed, "that they also may be one in us" (John 17:21). He wants them unified in love and purpose (John 13:35; Romans 15:5-7; I Corinthians 12:12-27; Ephesians 4:16).

Christ's gift to the Church included teachers and evangelists (Ephesians 4:11, 12). This is true not only of the local church but of the Body of Christ as a whole. God in recent years has raised up great interdenominational organizations to further the work of spreading the Gospel. There are faith mission boards, Bible institutes, seminaries, Gospel radio and TV programs, Christian publishers and Bible translators that all merit your fellowship through prayer and gifts. They are as much a part of the Body of Christ as the local church and are not in competition with it, but co-workers. "And the eye cannot say unto the hand, I have no need of thee: nor again the head to the feet, I have no need of you. . . . And whether one member suffer, all the members suffer with it; or one member be honored, all the members rejoice with it. Now ye are the body of Christ, and members in particular" (I Corinthians 12:21, 26, 27).

Your love and fellowship should not stop there, but should go on to the uttermost part of the earth, to the newly converted native who will some day share eternity with you and your Lord.

MEMORY HELPS

You are in the center (Luke 6:38).

The First Circle—Your family; prayer partner.

Second Circle—Your church; church group (I Corinthians 1:9; Hebrews 10:25).

Third Circle—Interdenominational schools; missions; Gospel radio and TV programs; Christian publishers.

Fourth Circle—The Body of Christ to the uttermost part of the earth (Matthew 28:19, 20).

As you view the whole scene, everything should be done as unto the Lord (Colossians 3:23).

Assignment:	Extra blessings:
I Corinthians 1:9	Luke 6:38
Colossians 3:23	Hebrews 10:25
II Corinthians 9:7, 8	Matthew 28:19, 20
	John 13:34, 35

QUESTIONS

1. Abraham and Joshua were too busy doing the work of God to have time for family worship (Gen. 18:19; Josh. 24:15). T ☐ F ☐

2. God holds parents responsible for training their children (Eph. 6:1-4). T ☐ F ☐

3. The Church—

   ☐ I Cor. 12:12, 13

   ☐ I Cor. 12:27

   ☐ Eph. 4:15

   (a) is called the Body of Christ
   (b) has Christ as the Head of the Body
   (c) has all "born-again" believers as members in particular of the Body

4. The word *church* is also used in the New Testament to refer to a local body of believers (Gal. 1:2; Philemon 1:2). T ☐ F ☐

5. The New Testament never tells Christians they should meet together for worship and instruction (Heb. 10:25). T ☐ F ☐

6. Hearing the Word preached will strengthen your faith and help you grow spiritually (Rom. 10:17; I Peter 2:2). T ☐ F ☐

7. I Thesssalonians 5:12, 13 teaches that your pastor and spiritual leaders should respect and esteem *you* highly. T ☐ F ☐

8. What will help keep unity in a church (Col. 3:14)? _____

9. Matthew 28:19, 20 teaches that the church's main commission is to raise the standard of living of people who are less fortunate than we are. **T F** ☐ ☐

10. The early church, according to Acts 2: 40-42; 13:1-3, preached, baptized, taught (continued in the apostles' doctrine), fellowshiped together, broke bread, prayed and sent out missionaries. **T F** ☐ ☐

11. II Corinthians 9:7 teaches you are to give—
    ☐ as you purpose in your heart, not grudgingly or of necessity but cheerfully.
    ☐ a tithe.
    ☐ what the church asks of you.

12. If you sow bountifully you will reap bountifully (II Cor. 9:6). **T F** ☐ ☐

13. Paul recommended that the church members at Corinth should lay up systematically and regularly on the first day of the week, if they had any money left after paying bills (I Cor. 16:2). **T F** ☐ ☐

14. Where are you told to lay up treasures (Matt. 6:20, 21)? _____

15. What did God give for you (John 3:16)? _____

16. What will He give you (Rom. 8:32; Phil. 4:19)? _____

17. Ephesians 2:8-10 teaches salvation is a gift, but you are created unto _____

18. Good works are unprofitable to the Christian (Titus 3:8). **T F** ☐ ☐

19. Colossians 3:23 teaches you should do all things as unto _____ and Matthew 5:16 teaches that it should bring glory to _____

20. What prepares a Christian for every good work (II Tim. 3:16, 17)? _____

If you do not have a prayer partner, have you started praying for one? _____ Are you an active member of a local church? _____ Are you making your "giving" a matter of prayer? _____ Are you praying that God will use you in His service? _____ How many chapters have you read in your Bible the past week? _____

Have you memorized I Cor. 1:9 _____; Col. 3:23 _____; II Cor. 9:7, 8? _____

Extra blessings: Luke 6:38 _____; Heb. 10:25 _____; Matt. 28:19, 20 _____; John 13:34, 35? _____

GROWING THROUGH FELLOWSHIP WITH GOD

GETTING TO "KNOW HIM"

You have met a Person, the Lord Jesus Christ, and have received Him as your Saviour. He gave you eternal life, *His life*. It is very important that you become better acquainted with Him as a Person. You are not concerned now with His gifts or His promises, but with His own self.

LIKE HIM

If two children spend a lot of time together, you will soon notice there are many things they do alike. They will both have certain expressions of speech, the same way of wearing their clothes, similar likes and dislikes, and other things they share in common. Christians, according to the purpose and desire of God, are to be conformed to the "image of his Son" (Romans 8:29; II Corinthians 3:18). One of the most effective ways to realize this is to set aside a time for fellowship with God each day.

Some husbands and wives have realized after a hasty courtship and marriage that they did not know each other very well. Their life partners had habits and interests which they were not aware of. It takes time to get to *know* someone. You have to spend much time together; and *you* need to spend time with God.

Our Spirit Thirsts

"And that which is born of the Spirit is spirit" (John 3:6). You are now a partaker of the divine nature (II Peter 1:4). Your spirit thirsts for fellowship with God. There is a place in your life for fellowship with other Christians, but there is also a place only God can fill. The better you know Christ, the easier it will be to tell others about *Him*.

An Amazing Fact

"The Father seeketh such to worship him" (John 4:23). It seems almost unbelievable that God would allow His creatures to fellowship with Him. But that He desires it, and that you could in any way bring pleasure to Him, is a fact that can be explained only by God. What an example of grace He has made you!

Let Us Not Forget—

There is only one reason you are now permitted to come into His presence. Jesus bore the penalty for your sins on the cross. He has now given you His perfect righteousness and the right to come in His name. Now you can come boldly (not irreverently but with confidence) to the throne of grace (Hebrews 4:16).

That You Might Know Him

You have already learned that the Holy Spirit dwells in the heart of every Christian. Now Jesus promises the obedient Christian that He will manifest (reveal) Himself to him, and that He and the Father will come and make their abode with him (John 14:21-23). God not only desires your fellowship, but He wants to manifest or reveal Himself to you. He wants you to *know Him.*

Engaged

 When a young couple are engaged their times together are very precious to them. If they are separated for a while, they miss each other and long for the time when they can be reunited. If the young lady should start ignoring or avoiding the young man, or become too busy to see him, he would know something was wrong. Perhaps she does not love him or has met someone she loves more.

THE BRIDE OF CHRIST

The Bible teaches that the Church is the Bride of Christ (Ephesians 5:25-27; Revelation 19:7; 21:9). You are betrothed to Him. He wants to spend time with you. But how easy it is to be "too busy"! Christ rebuked the church at Ephesus because it had left its first love (Revelation 2:4). Let us realize that Christ longs to have fellowship with us.

THE QUIET TIME

Establishing a *quiet time* is one of the most important steps you can take. It will help you grow more spiritually in the time involved than anything else you can do. It is the doorway into the *abundant life.* You cannot afford *not* to have a *quiet time.*

4 THINGS

Good intentions are all right but often they do not get the job done. If you just *intend* to have a little time with the Lord after you finish all the rest of the work, you will probably *never* establish a *quiet time.*

MAKE TIME

Be definite. Early in the day is usually best. It is difficult to say what time is best for everyone. Jobs, duties and temperaments differ. Some will find early morning before breakfast best, others after breakfast or late at night, or at some other time during the day. Perhaps a mother's

best time is after the children are off to school
or when the baby is asleep. If at all possible,
try to meet with God before you meet the problems of the day.

If you can arrange to eat three times a day
to meet the needs of your body, you can arrange
a time each day to meet the needs of your soul.

How Much Time

Start with no less than 15 minutes. Then
guard it jealously. You may increase it as the
Lord leads. Make this a regular part of your
daily program.

Is it too much to ask 1/96th of every 24 hours?
Stop right now and decide on a time. Promise
it to the Lord. Now remember that He, your
Bridegroom, will be waiting to keep His date
with you. Do not disappoint Him!

A Definite Place

Lovers usually have a favorite place where
they can be alone. If at all possible find a quiet
place to meet with the Lover of your soul. This
may be a problem for some people. Perhaps you
can prepare a closet, a storage room, a place in
the basement, in the garage or in the yard. Decide right now where you can have your *quiet
time* with the Lord.

A Definite Aim

Your desire is to grow more Christlike through
fellowship with God. You want to "know him
[as a Person], and the *power* of his resurrection,

and the fellowship of his sufferings, being made conformable unto his death" (Philippians 3:10). You want Him actually to live His life through you (Galatians 2:20).

You not only want to know Him, but want Him to show you yourself as He sees you. Your *quiet time* should be a time for self-examination, confession and cleansing.

You wish to share His thoughts and desires. You want to acknowledge your complete dependence upon Him and bring to Him your need for wisdom, guidance and material necessities, so you may be strengthened and prepared to meet the temptations and problems of the day (Isaiah 40:29-31).

A METHOD

Your quiet time should have three main ingredients: the Word, meditation and prayer. They will be intermingled or blended. Do not plan in too great detail, but on the other hand do not just wander around and waste time. The following method is suggested to help you use the Bible in your *quiet time*.

"SPECS"

Many people find it necessary to wear glasses. Your prayer should be that of the psalmist: "Open thou mine eyes, that I may behold wondrous things out of thy law" (Psalm 119:18).

You need to put on your spiritual "specs" to see yourself as God sees you. So the Holy Spirit can use the Bible to search your heart and point

 out your sins. "For the word of God is quick, and powerful, and sharper than any twoedged sword, piercing even to the dividing asunder of soul and spirit, and of the joints and marrow, and is a discerner of the *thoughts* and *intents* of the heart. Neither is there any creature that is not *manifest* in his sight: but *all things* are naked and opened unto the eyes of him with whom we have to do" (Hebrews 4:12, 13). The Bible is also described as a glass (mirror) in which you can see yourself (James 1:23, 24). You want to see yourself as God sees you, and want the Holy Spirit to use the Word to reveal Christ to you. From Genesis to Revelation you have Christ pictured in types, symbols and promises.

You are not using the Bible now to gain information but as a means through which God can speak to you. He may use a verse to bring something to your attention entirely different than what the verse itself says, as a probe for your memory or conscience perhaps.

Do not hurry. Take a chapter or a portion of a chapter and go over it slowly, asking yourself these questions:

What—

  S in is there for me to forsake?
  P romise is there for me to claim?
  E xample is there for me to follow?
  C ommand for me to obey?
  S tumbling block or error to avoid?

What new thought do I have about God?

Included with this lesson is a sample "specs" on Colossians 3 to help you understand how to use them. Many more thoughts could be gained from this chapter but only a few have been entered so you may note the general plan. (You can use it for a pattern to make additional forms from notebook paper.) Paul's Epistles and the Proverbs are especially good to use. Do Colossians 3 first, and then go through other short books of the New Testament.

Suggestions for Using "Specs"

Make as short a note as possible; remember no one else need understand it. Do not try to answer the questions in order, but keep them all in mind. In some portions you may not find any *example* to follow but there may be many *promises* to claim, or the other way around.

When the Holy Spirit points out some sin, stop and confess it to God at once. Call it the same thing He does—gossiping, covetousness, unforgiveness or lying. They claim the forgiveness and cleansing of I John 1:9.

When you come to a *promise,* stop and claim it by faith and thank Him for it.

When you come to a *command,* stop and surrender to His will.

Look for the things that reveal the personality of Christ. This passage, Colossians 3:13 speaks of the forgiveness of Christ.

YOUR PERSONAL APPLICATION

Now that the Holy Spirit has revealed some new things concerning God's will for your life, what are you going to do about it? God has thrown some light on your pathway. *Obedience* means *happiness* (John 13:17) Disobedience or ignoring it is *sin* (James 4:17). Be definite. Suppose the Holy Spirit through Colossians 3:13 reveals that you have been unforgiving toward a neighbor; confess this sin to God. Tell your neighbor as soon as possible that you have forgiven him and ask forgiveness for your own unforgiving spirit; verse 20, disobedient or inconsiderate to parents—tell them or write your appreciation of them; verse 9, lying—pray that God will help you control your tongue this week, etc. Write it down, be definite. "Meditate upon these things; give thyself wholly to them; that thy profiting may appear to all" (I Timothy 4:15). *Meditation is spiritual digestion.* Put these things to work in your own life; make them a part of you.

A STRONG DEVOTIONAL LIFE

There is nothing more important to you as a Christian than to build a strong devotional life. It is the heartbeat of your spiritual life. Hiding God's Word in your heart and spending time alone with Him will prepare you for victory when you meet temptation, suffering, sorrow, and the problems that come your way. This is important.

Parallel Passages

As you become more familiar with your Bible one verse may remind you of another, or add a little information, or explain another one to you. You may want to write the reference in the margin of your Bible so you will not forget it. This is good practice in your regular Bible study. Make your Bible its own best commentary but do not become too preoccupied with this during your *quiet time*.

Praise

Take time to honor and praise God. Meditate upon His goodness, His love, and His mercy, and thank Him for the grace He has bestowed upon you. The Bible says that whoever offers praise glorifies God. Spend time reading and meditating in the Psalms. These are the heart cries of God's people.

Petitions and Intercessions

After your heart has been cleansed by the Word, as Ephesians 5:26 reveals, bring your requests to God for yourself and others. Guidance, strength, wisdom, clothes, food, all your *needs* have been promised to you. As you do your "specs," start a list of things God has impressed on your heart to pray for. You already have a list of unsaved loved ones and friends for whom you are praying (Lesson 4). The next lesson will have some suggestions for the use of prayer lists for more effective and definite praying.

GUARANTEED PRAYER

A father and his son are out walking and the father might say to the little boy, "Would you like an ice-cream cone?" Or, "Shall we buy some flowers to take home to Mother?" The son says, "Yes, I would like an ice-cream cone." Or, "Yes, let's get Mother some flowers." The little boy had not been thinking of these things. The suggestion comes entirely from the father. The father could have just bought these things. He had plenty of money, and there was a place to buy them, but that was not the way he wanted to do it.

GOD WORKS THROUGH PRAYER, AND "PRAYER
    CHANGES THINGS"

There is a level of fellowship and communion with God where prayer becomes *guaranteed prayer*. It is not for the careless, indifferent Christian who never learns to fellowship and spend time with God.

TRUE PRAYER

True prayer starts in Heaven in the mind and heart of God. Through the Holy Spirit, and usually the Word, God suggests His desire for you. You ask for it; the Holy Spirit takes up our request and presents it in the name of the Son; and God answers. This is what is meant by prayer in the Spirit (Ephesians 6:18; Jude 20). That is why some men have such power in prayer. Their prayers are Spirit-suggested. For instance, Elijah prayed that it would not rain. For three and a half years it did not rain until he prayed for rain. It was the thing God wished to do. He had found a co-worker on earth.

True prayer is more than just "getting" God to do something. It is "letting" Him do things for you and others through your Spirit-led prayers.

Many Christians have testified that without any previous thought they have been impressed to pray for some friend, a member of the family, or a missionary. Later they have learned that God supernaturally worked in their behalf. The object of their prayers was delivered from temptation, or distress, or danger, or persecution, or the power of Satan, or received Christ as Saviour. God works through prayer. That is His chosen way of doing things. He had found a co-worker who was living in close fellowship with Him. Someone that could be led by the Holy Spirit in prayer. Would you like to be a co-worked with God?

An airplane is flying toward a big city and encounters a storm. The pilot is concerned for the safety of his passengers, so he radios ahead for information and instructions. The airport radios back the information and the flight is continued. The pilot can adjust his radio to receive the programs that are being broadcast, and all kinds of unknown and unsought information will come in. It will be limited only by the amount of time he spends at his radio set.

Some Christians never get beyond the level of petitions, or just asking. God has something better for you. There is a fellowship and communion with God where He will reveal His thoughts, desires and plans. Just as God, after fellowshiping with Abraham, said: "Shall I hide from Abraham that thing which I do?" (Genesis 18:17). Adjust your life and spend time with God that you might be used to His honor and glory.

MORE QUIET-TIME SUGGESTIONS—

1. Praying out loud will often keep your thoughts from wandering. It will help you to pray before others, so you will not be afraid of the sound of your own voice.

2. Do not get into a rut; vary your routine if you find it hard to concentrate.

3. Expect the presence of God; He has promised to be there (John 14:16; Matthew 28:20).

4. If you miss a day, do not let that ruin your day. Commune with Him at work or in school. Claim His power to use the day to glorify Him. If it is your fault, confess it to Him.

5. Make sure your attitude is right.

6. Do not use this time to prepare your Sunday school lesson or Bible talk for your study group or circle meeting.

"Open thou mine eyes"
(Psalm 119:18).

Passage _____

Date _____

S ins to forsake—

P romises to claim—

E xamples to follow—

C ommands to obey—

S tumbling blocks or errors to avoid—

New thoughts about God—

Personal application of the Word to *my* life—

"Open thou mine eyes"
(Psalm 119:18).

Passage _Colossians 3_

Date _July 19_

S ins to forsake— *v. 8, anger; v. 9, lying;*
v. 13, unforgiving; v. 15, worry,
unthankful; v. 17, working for self-glory;

P romises to claim— *v. 4, be with Christ;*
v. 13, His forgiveness; v. 25, reward.

E xamples to follow— *v. 25, Christ's*
forgiveness.

C ommands to obey— *vv. 8, 12, 14; vv. 18-*
21 love my family; v. 23, do all
things as unto God.

S tumbling blocks or errors to avoid— *v. 2*
love of earthly things; v. 8, works of the
flesh; v. 11, discrimination.

New thoughts about God— *v. 13, Christ's*
forgiveness is my example.

Personal application of the Word to my life—
1. Ask God's help in controlling my tongue
2. Ask my neighbor's forgiveness
3. Write to parents
4. Cast my cares on God and not
worry.   *I Peter 5:7*

MEMORY HELPS

As you read and meditate upon the Word, the Holy Spirit will use it to show you—

—Yourself as God sees you (Hebrews 4:12)

—Christ
Philippians 3:10
(Luke 24:27)

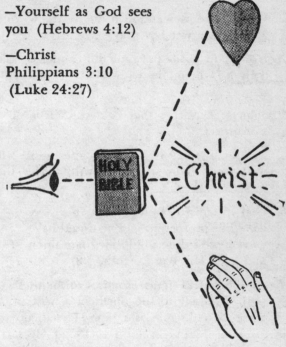

Meditate
I Timothy 4:15

—What to pray for
Jude 20

Assignment:
Hebrews 4:12
Philippians 3:10
I Timothy 4:15

Extra blessings:
II Corinthians 3:18
Jude 20
Luke 24:27

QUESTIONS

1. Part of your prayer time should be secret prayer between you and God (Matt. 6:6).   T F   ☐ ☐

2. What place is mentioned in Matthew 26:36 where Jesus went to pray? _____

3. How many periods of time did Daniel set aside daily to commune with God (Dan. 6:10)?

   _____

4. John 4:23 teaches that God seeks true worshipers.   T F   ☐ ☐

5. In Isaiah 40:29-31 God promises those who wait upon Him that He will renew their

   _____

6. God promised Joshua that his way would be prosperous and he would have good success if he would meditate upon and keep His Word. (Josh. 1:8).   T F   ☐ ☐

7. In John 14:21 Jesus promises to manifest (reveal) Himself to the obedient Christian. In verse 22 a disciple asks how He will do this. In verse 26 and in John 16:13, 14 He says it is by the _____ who will teach you and glorify Christ.

8. You can sometimes fool men by your deeds, but the Holy Spirit can use the Word of God to show you the real _____ and _____ of our hearts (Heb. 4:12).

9. How should you regard the thoughts and truths the Holy Spirit reveals (Ps. 139:17)? _____

   _____

10. The Bible says

☐ Eph. 6:18   (a) commit thy way unto the Lord

☐ Prov. 15:8, 29   (b) true prayer should be guided by the Holy Spirit

☐ Jer. 29:13   (c) sin hinders prayer

☐ Isa. 59:1, 2   (d) the prayers of the upright are a delight to the Lord

☐ Ps. 37:4, 5   (e) should seek the Lord with your whole heart

11. In Acts 13:1-4 the Holy Spirit impressed His message on a praying church and _____ and Saul were sent on their first missionary journey.

12. I Timothy 4:15 teaches that meditation   **T F** is a waste of time.   ☐ ☐

13. What four things must you decide on when you start a quiet time? _____
_____   _____
_____

14. Have you done a "Specs" as recommended in the lesson? _____ After you have completed a few of them, you can do them mentally and only write out the personal applications to your life.

15. How many days have you had a quiet time during the past week? _____
How many chapters in the Bible have you read? _____

Have you memorized Heb. 4:12; _____;
Phil. 3:10 _____; I Tim. 4:15? _____

Extra blessings: II Cor. 3:18 _____; Jude 20
_____; Luke 24:27? _____

LESSON 10

FOLLOWING DIRECTIONS

GOD'S WILL

The personnel manager of a large company calls together a group of new employees to assign their duties. Part of them he sends to a technical training school. Others he assigns to older employees to train "on the job." There are many different departments in the company. There is an advertising department which informs people about the product; demonstrators who show the people how it can be used; door-to-door salesmen who take the product right to the people; other salesmen who sell in wholesale quantities; and troubleshooters who help new customers, those who are having difficulty, or do not understand how to use the product. Each department is important to the company.

GOD'S WILL FOR YOU—Read I Corinthians 12:1-27

When you were saved you became a member of the Body of Christ (vv. 12, 13). Gifts of the Spirit of God have been given to *every* one, and it is according as *God* wills (v. 11).

Everyone is not an eye or an ear. But God has a purpose and a plan for every member. It is a place for which God has equipped you to work. Some are places of obscurity, working behind the scenes, unknown to the world.

Jesus said: "Ye shall be witnesses unto me . . . unto the uttermost part of the earth" (Acts 1:8). This is the job of the Body of Christ. Where is your place? All God's callings are important in His program for the evangelization of the world. Your main concern should be to find God's will for your life. That will be the happiest way, if you accept it, to spend your life on this earth.

After awhile the personnel manager might transfer one of the workers to another department. Extra help might have been needed in the first department to finish a certain task, or the employee needed to understand those duties to equip him for more efficient work in another department. The employees do not wander from job to job but are assigned to their positions. The manager is very careful never to assign any worker to a task he is unable to do.

NEW ASSIGNMENTS

After the worker becomes acquainted with the product and the company's method of operation, the manager calls him into his office and presents a new job to him. He probably will not be forced to take it, but if he does not he might miss a big opportunity. Until he is willing to do what he is asked, he cannot be of much use to the company. Someone else must do the job he was asked to do. If he agrees to do the job the manager will provide all the help needed.

A Place to Work

Suppose the employee is to work as a demonstrator-salesman. The company wants him to do as good a job as possible. They give him a book which in a general way sets down the manner in which he is to conduct himself. They arrange for him to meet other employees along the way. They send him new instructions and information by mail. They send the field representative with him to train him. Then they tell him, "If you run into a problem you cannot solve, call us on the telephone and we will help you."

The Book Says—

The book the company has given the employee is very definite about some things. It says, "Never lie about the product." "Always be courteous." Sometimes the worker might not remember whether or not the book has instructions regarding a certain thing and he will have to look it up. If the book speaks plainly, he will not need to look any further.

It Is Not in the Book

Every decision to be made will not be listed in the book. Usually there will be certain principles which will fit every problem.

Call the Home Office

If he does not know what to do the worker can call the home office and ask for instructions. He might be advised that the case in question is similar to the situation on a certain page in the book.

Advice

If the field representative is on hand to advise him, the worker should always listen closely and follow instructions very carefully. The representative will never tell him to do something contrary to the book.

Circumstances

His territory might not look good to him. He might doubt if he will ever sell anything. This is not his responsibility. As long as he knows he is where he is supposed to be, and doing his job the best he can, he should leave the results to the home office. If the employee is faithful to the first task, he will then be given added responsibility. The company will be pleased to have a man on whom they can depend.

PEOPLE GOD HAS BEEN ABLE TO USE

God records in His Word some characteristics and attitudes of the people He has been able to use in the past.

Samuel—

When God called to Samuel he said: "Speak; for thy servant heareth" (I Samuel 3:10). He considered himself a servant and was eager to know what God wanted.

Isaiah—

When the Lord said: "Whom shall I send, and who will go for us?" Isaiah did not wait to ask what the task was but said: "Here am I; send me" (Isaiah 6:8, 9).

Joshua—

God told Joshua to be obedient in the things he already knew were His will and his way would be prosperous (Joshua 1:8, 9).

Noah—

Noah "walked with God" (Genesis 6:9). Later in verse 14, God tells him to build the ark. We must walk in fellowship with God to enable Him to guide and use us. In Lesson 5 you were asked to present yourself to God and to be filled by the Holy Spirit. This step cannot be skipped if God is to use you. (Review Lesson 5.)

STUDY THE FOLLOWING PROMISES

God has a plan—Psalm 37:23:

"The steps of a good man are ordered by the Lord: and he delighteth in his way."

God promises to guide you—Psalm 32:8:

"I will instruct thee and teach thee in the way which thou shalt go: I will guide thee with mine eye."

Three steps to guidance—Proverbs 3:5, 6:

1. "Trust in the Lord with all thine heart; and
2. Lean not unto thine own understanding.
3. In all thy ways acknowledge him, *and He shall direct thy paths.*"

If you ask, He will give you wisdom—James 1:5:

"If any of you lack wisdom, let him ask of God, that giveth to all men liberally, and upbraideth not; and it shall be given him."

Three steps to know His will—Romans 12:1, 2:

1. "Present your bodies . . . unto God. . . .
2. Be not conformed to this world: but
3. Be ye transformed by the renewing of your mind, *That ye may prove what is that good, and acceptable, and perfect will of God.*"

YOU CAN MISS GOD'S PLAN FOR YOU

As God gives the opportunity to serve Him, be faithful and accept His leading. God will not *force* you to fit into His plan. Through sin or neglect you can miss His first choice for you. His plan is the life of blessing, the *abundant life*. God may have to turn to someone else to do the work He planned for you. This happened to Moses (Exodus 3:10-12; 4:10-16) ; it could have happened to Queen Esther (Esther 4:14) . There are some things about which God wants you to exercise your own free will and obey Him. There are other things He commands you to do. If you know it is God's will, do it or He may have to chasten you. (Read the Book of Jonah.)

TYPES OF GUIDANCE

You need guidance of two types. First you need to know in what general direction to start. It must be connected with the evangelization of the world because that is what Christ commanded. Then you need light on your path to take the next step. Too often Christians spend all their time and effort seeking a telescope to tell in minute detail what the future holds for them. In reality their big need is a light to keep them from stumbling day by day. In the last lesson you started a *quiet time* to help guide you in both ways.

SOURCES OF GUIDANCES—

THE WORD OF GOD

"Thy word is a lamp unto my feet, and a light unto my path" (Psalm 119:105) . The will of God is revealed very definitely about many things

 in the Bible. For example, it is always wrong to lie. The more familiar you become with the Bible the more you will understand what God would have you do. You do not need to ask for guidance when His will is clearly revealed in His Word. It is the final authority. If you do not know what the Bible says about a certain thing, look it up in a concordance.

PRINCIPLES IN THE WORD

You can pray that God will use His Word to direct your thinking. God has set down many principles in it. A decision for almost every situation can be made on these principles. God has promised wisdom (James 1:5). This does not mean you can open the Bible at random, put your finger on a verse and God will use it as a guide. First, you must be walking in fellowship with Him, keeping your quiet time. You must not rush into His presence only in time of need. Then as you read, expect the Holy Spirit to impress a verse or portion on your heart.

THE LEADING OF THE HOLY SPIRIT

You have Someone much wiser than the field representative in our story—the Holy Spirit dwelling in your heart. It is His business to lead you (Romans 8:14). One of the easiest ways for Him to guide you is through the verses you have memorized. They are always with you so He can use them. "Walk in the Spirit, and ye shall not fulfill the lust of the flesh" (Galatians 5:16).

IMPRESSIONS

There are times when the Holy Spirit speaks to the spiritual Christian by deep-seated impressions. In your heart you will know whether or not God wants you to do something. It might be the choice between two different jobs. From all outward appearances they might seem equal. But each time you consider one, an uneasy feeling comes over you.

How can you tell the difference between your feelings and the leading of the Holy Spirit? Feelings are as changeable as the weather. Today you are happy; tomorrow you are sad. The impressions of the Holy Spirit will remain.

CAUTION! REMEMBER—

There will never be any guidance contrary to the Word of God. Usually it will be through the use of the Word. It will always be in perfect harmony with the Word, or it will not be divine guidance.

CLOSED DOORS

Sometimes you may have several ways open to you and not know which way to go, but a decision must be made. Pray that God will close the door if it is not His will and then start in

that direction. If it is not His will expect Him 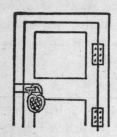 to close the door. He guided Paul this way. (Read Acts 16:6-10.) A problem may arise. How can you tell if it is God closing a door or if it is the opposition of Satan? If God is closing the door there will be peace in your heart about it. He also will probably give you further guidance as He did Paul. Here too you must be in close fellowship with Him. You must be sensitive to His leading. This can be obtained only by spending time with Him and His Word. Do not neglect your daily quiet time.

CIRCUMSTANCES, CONDITIONS AND SURROUNDINGS

Something may happen that will not seem reasonable to you. It happened to Joseph. God showed him in a dream that He had an important position for him (Genesis 37:5-10). While a boy he was sold as a slave and later found himself in prison unjustly. It would seem that he was out of the will of God, but the Bible says, "The Lord was with him" (Genesis 39:1, 2). Joseph knew later it was God who sent him to Egypt (Genesis 45:5-7; 50:20). Regardless of the circumstances, if you are in fellowship with God, and He is "with you," take courage. Commit yourself to Him; it is His responsibility.

UP THE LADDER OF USEFULNESS

If you are faithful in the little things God asks you to do, you will become usable for bigger responsibilities. The Bible gives the example of Philip.

1. He was chosen as a deacon (Acts 6:5).
2. Next, we find him in Samaria preaching (Acts 8:5).
3. God had found a man who would obey Him. He sent him to lead the Ethiopian eunuch to Christ (Acts 8:26-40).
4. Twenty-five years later he is mentioned as Philip the evangelist, living at Caesarea (Acts 21:8). He lived a life of fruitful service for Christ.

WHAT SHALL YOU DO WITH YOUR LIFE?

Remember the job of the church is evangelization of the world. Find out what the needs are in your neighborhood, your city, your state, your nation, other nations, and the uttermost part of the world. Start praying about these needs. Ask God what part He would have you play. You cannot go everywhere, but every place is important in God's sight.

TRAINING

As God impresses a type of service upon your heart, find out what training you will need to be most effective. Christ's gifts to the church include pastors and teachers (Ephesians 4:11). Everyone should study (II Timothy 2:15). Pray about your training. What kind it should be and where you should get it.

Gifts of the Spirit and Talents—I Corinthians 12:5-7, 11

Do not confuse natural talents and the gifts of the Holy Spirit. God's work is done in God's power. This is what God tried to tell Moses (Exodus 4:10-12). God has often chosen weak and common things to do His work (I Corinthians 1:27) so the glory will go to God and not to man (II Corinthians 4:7; 12:9). Your natural talents and abilities must be empowered by the Holy Spirit to be used by God (John 15:5).

Suggestions in Finding God's Will—

1. Surrender your own will.
2. Seek the Spirit's will through the Word.
3. Note providential circumstances.
4. Pray for guidance.
5. Wait on God until you can make a decision and have peace in your heart about it.

Balance Sheet

Some Christians use what they call a balance sheet. They take a blank sheet of paper and divide it in half. On one side of the paper they write all the factors in favor of the proposition, and on the other side all the factors against it. They prayerfully go over the list for several days, adding new thoughts to either side and crossing out the ones that do not seem important after praying about them. Sooner or later there is an impression upon the heart as to what course to take. If the impression remains and intensifies after continued prayer, they proceed in that direction. A word of caution—only those walking in close fellowship with God can expect to know God's will. A carnal Christian is not using the light he has.

EXPENSE ACCOUNT

When the salesman in our story went on the road to represent his company, they put him on an expense account plus his salary. They wanted him to have the clothes he needed, so he would make a good impression as he represented the company. They paid for his meals and the hotel bill. If he needed a car, samples, or anything else to perform his job, they would provide it to further the interests of the company. They would not pay for luxuries he might want for his own pleasure. The book of rules they gave him listed the expenses the company would honor.

AMBASSADORS FOR CHRIST—II Corinthians 5:20

You are representing Christ here on earth. You are to evangelize the world in His stead.

A HEAVENLY EXPENSE ACCOUNT—Matthew 6:25-33

"But seek ye first the kingdom of God, and

his righteousness; and all these things shall be added unto you." God in His Word has given us many promises. Real prayer puts its finger upon some promise of God and then asks Him to be faithful to His Word.

Included with this lesson is a page to list your prayer requests and a sample page. Their use is encouraged for the following reasons:

1. To make you more definite in prayer.
2. To make you more effective in your prayer life.
3. To show the faithfulness of God as He answers your prayers.
4. To help your memory.
5. To help keep your thoughts from wandering during prayer time.

REQUESTS FOR YOUR PRAYER LIST

1. The list of unsaved people God has placed on your heart. (You were asked to make a list in Lesson 4.) Other people such as your family, Sunday school class, pastor, missionaries, and your neighbors.
2. Christian organizations, such as churches, schools, missions, or Gospel radio programs.
3. Definite requests for your personal life.
4. The other suggestions in this lesson.

DO NOT—

Make your list so long it becomes a burden

Pray to the prayer list

Get into a rut; change your routine in your *quiet time* occasionally. If your list gets too long, divide it up into different days or set aside more time for prayer. Periodically go through your list and cross out the requests for which you no longer have a burden.

Remember—*prayer is God's way of doing things for you.*

PRAYER

(Keeping accounts with God—a record of His faithfulness)

Date	Request	Scripture Promise	Date Answered
Aug. 6	Joe - be saved	II Peter 3:9	
Aug. 30	New shoes	Matt. 6:33	Sept. 3
Aug. 31	Not to worry about K.N.T.O.	I Peter 5:7	Yes
Sept. 7	Wisdom in my studies	James 1:5	
Sept. 10	Boldness to witness to J.	Acts 4:29	Sept. 11
Sept. 15	Message for Bible class and courage to give it	Phil. 4:13	Sept. 22
Sept. 16	I might not resent B, but love him	Gal. 5:22,23	
Sept. 18	A way to C.A.S.H.D.	Phil. 4:19	

Some requests may be of a personal nature and you may want to abbreviate them. Remember these pages are for your own use, but you may want to share them with your prayer partner, or show some new Christian how to use them.

Besides the sample requests above, you might have some of a general nature that you need not write down.

MEMORY HELPS

Guidance

Not thine own understanding
Proverbs 3:5, 6
Jeremiah 10:23

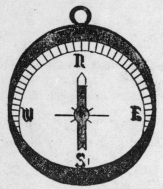

By the
Psa. 119:105
Word and the
Wisdom of God
James 1:5

By the
Eye of God
Psa. 32:8

By the
Spirit of God
Galatians 5:16
John 16:13

Assignment:
 Proverbs 3:5, 6
 James 1:5
 Galatians 5:16
 Psalm 32:8

Extra blessings:
 Psalm 119:105
 Jeremiah 10:23
 John 16:13

QUESTIONS

1. Man must have the Lord's guidance to
   live in a manner pleasing to Him (Jer. T F
   10:23).   ☐ ☐

2. Who is to lead and guide the Christian (Rom.
   8:14; John 16:13)? _____

3. In II Samuel 22:31 David says the way of God
   is—
   - ☐ perfect
   - ☐ hard
   - ☐ easy

4. The Christian's first duty is to obey the T F
   king or ruler over him (Acts 5:29).   ☐ ☐

5. Luke 6:46 teaches that if you call Jesus Lord
   and claim Him as your Saviour you should
   - ☐ go to church regularly
   - ☐ give to the poor
   - ☐ do the things He asks

6. John 13:17 says if you live according to God's
   will, you can expect your life to be _____
   _____

7. A Christian is supposed to conform his
   life to the pattern of the world around T F
   him (Rom. 12:2).   ☐ ☐

8. In trying to decide what is the proper thing
   for you, as a Christian, to do concerning things
   not particularly mentioned in the Bible, it is
   sometimes helpful to ask yourself—

   ☐ I Cor. 10:31   (a) can I do this in the
                         name of Christ
   ☐ Col. 3:17   (b) does it have the ap-
                         pearance of evil

☐ I Thess. 5:22

☐ Rom. 14:13

☐ Col. 1:10

☐ II Cor. 5:10

(c) will this bring glory to God

(d) should an ambassador do this

(e) is this walking worthy of the Lord

(f) will this cause my brother to stumble

9. Psalm 119:105 says one source of guidance is the _____

10. If you ask Him will God guide you (Ps. 32:8)? _____

11. If it is really God guiding you, it will not be contrary to the _____

12. Sometimes _____ may close a door or make it impossible to go contrary to His wishes (Acts 16:6-10).

13. Circumstances may seem unreasonable, but if you are in God's will you will be like Joseph and know by the witness in your heart that _____ is with you (Gen. 39:1, 2).

14. Have you read I Cor. 12:1-27 _____; Acts 16:6-10 _____; the Book of Jonah? _____

15. Have you started a prayer list? _____

How many days of the past week have you had a *quiet time?* _____ How many chapters of your Bible have you read? _____ Have you memorized Prov. 3:5, 6 _____; James 1:5 _____; Gal. 5:16 _____; Ps. 32:8? _____

Extra blessings: Ps. 119:105 _ _____; Jer. 10:23 _____; John 16:13? _____

LESSON 11

FISHING

CO-LABORERS WITH GOD

Jesus said: "Follow me, and I will make you fishers of men" (Matthew 4:19). Notice they were only required to *follow* Him. It was His responsibility to make them fishers of men.

Jesus gradually revealed His plan for His followers. It is our responsibility to be witnesses "to every creature" (Mark 16:15) and to "the uttermost part of the earth" (Acts 1:8). This command was not given to only the apostles, or to a few missionaries, or to preachers, or to Sunday school teachers, but to every Christian. Jesus said: "Follow me, and I *will make you fishers of men.*" Are you following? Then you should be fishing.

Although the disciples were with Jesus about three years, they did not wait until Jesus returned to Heaven to start fishing. Many people try to excuse themselves by saying, "I do not know enough to lead someone to Christ." This is not true. *If you know enough to be saved, you know enough to lead another person to Christ.* As soon as Andrew had found Jesus he brought Peter to Him; and Philip brought Nathanael. The Samaritan woman was not a disciple; in fact she was from the lowest level of society, yet she was the means by which many people from her city came to Jesus (John 4:39).

GOING FISHING

A father takes his little boy fishing. There are many places they could go but the father selects a little lake near their home. This is the first time the boy has been permitted to go along and he is very excited. His father has made all the preparations. They have all the fishing tackle and equipment they will need. The father knows what kind of fish are in the lake, so he has brought the right kind of poles, lines, and hooks of just the right size.

BAIT

All fish do not feed on the same thing, but the father is a wise fisherman so he has selected the right kinds of bait for the fish in this lake. When they get to the lake, the father picks the particular spot where they will fish. He shows his son which bait to use and how to bait the hook and cast it out on the water where the fish are. After following his father's instructions the boy has a "bite" on the line. Even though he wants to, he is unable to land the fish by himself and his father must help him pull it in. After he gets a little older, he may go up on the mountain stream or out on the ocean to fish. Although the method will vary some, there are certain principles that are true of all types of fishing. The important thing for the son to do is to follow his father's instructions.

Must Follow

Jesus taught His disciples many things to equip them for the job He had for them. They learned to pray; He helped them understand the Scriptures; and He promised the Holy Spirit would help them (Luke 11:1; 24:45; Acts 1:8).

In the preceding lessons you have been studying the same things. It is very important that you walk in close fellowship with God so you can know and follow His instructions as you fish for men, for if you have been sincere and are really "following" He will make you a "fisher of men."

If you want to be used by God do not neglect your *quiet time* and private devotional life.

Hide the Word in your heart; it is the sword of the Spirit (Ephesians 6:17). Keep reviewing the verses in your spare time.

Where Shall You Start?

The first thing is to ask God to guide you to someone. Pray about the people right around you who are lost. It might be someone in your own family, your neighbor, or someone where you work. God will probably use you where you are before He takes you somewhere else.

THE GOSPEL

What spiritual "bait" will you use? The Gospel (the good news) is the *bait* of the fisher of men. The Gospel is not just a system of ethics, an organization, or doing things. The heart of the Gospel is a Person, and the work He has done for you. It is the Lord Jesus Christ, the Son of God, the Saviour who was promised, who "died for our sins . . . was buried and . . . rose again the third day according to the scriptures" (I Corinthians 15:3, 4). It is His eternal life that is offered to the sinner (I John 5:11, 12).

THE METHOD

Just as the fisherman puts the bait into the water so the fish can see it, the fisher of men must introduce Christ to the lost. The simplest and one of the most effective methods is just telling others how you came to know Him and how He has met the need in your life. It is like introducing one friend to another.

Help people understand that becoming a *Christ*ian is not doing something, but is receiving some*one*, the Person Jesus Christ.

Keep yourself in the ba_kground; it is Christ you are presenting, not yourself.

THE TACKLE—THE WORD

What kind of "tackle" will the fisher of men use? A fisherman does not just throw the bait on the water. The Bible says: "Being born again, not of corruptible seed, but of incorruptible, by the word of God, which liveth and abideth forever" (I Peter 1:23). It makes no difference whether the fish thinks the line is "no good" or that the hook will not hold it. The line has been tested and will do the job. Some people say they do not believe God's Word, but it has also been tested. God promises that "the word of God is quick, and powerful, and sharper than any two-edged sword . . . and is a discerner of the thoughts and intents of the heart" (Hebrews 4:12). "Is not my word like as a fire? saith the Lord; and like a hammer that breaketh the rock in pieces?" (Jeremiah 23:29) "It shall not return unto me void, but it shall accomplish that which I please, and it shall prosper in the thing whereto I sent it" (Isaiah 55:11). Do not argue about the Word, or defend it—*use it*.

LANDING YOUR CATCH

Just as the little boy had to have help to pull in his fish, you must have help to land your man for Christ. The Bible teaches that the seed is the Word, and through the work of the Holy Spirit, a person is "born again" (John 3:3-6). No matter how hard you try, landing your man

must be through the power of the Holy Spirit. It is through consecrated individuals, people who are filled with the Holy Spirit, that He works. "But ye shall receive power, after that the Holy Ghost is come upon you: and ye shall be witnesses unto me" (Acts 1:8).

"And when he [the Holy Spirit] is come, he will reprove the world of sin, and of righteousness, and of judgment" (John 16:8). It is through believers that He works. "God was in Christ, reconciling the world unto himself." He has finished the work of salvation, and now "hath committed unto us the word of reconciliation. Now then we are ambassadors for Christ, as though God did beseech you *by us;* we pray you in *Christ's stead,* be ye reconciled to God" (II Corinthians 5:19, 20). To be effective our words, our thoughts, our attitudes, and our plans must be guided and controlled by the Holy Spirit; so we can go to the right person, say the right thing in the right way and at the right time. Unless you are led by the Holy Spirit, it will be an unfruitful waste of time and effort and might even harm the Lord's work (John 15:5).

DOOMED

Suppose the little lake where the boy and his

father went fishing was to be drained in a few
weeks. All the fish he and his father and other
people did not catch would die when the water
was gone, but his father had prepared a new
lake for their fish. Every person in this world is
under condemnation for his sins (John 3:18;
Romans 2:12). There is only one way of escape
—through the Lord Jesus (John 14:6; Acts
4:12).

Two Main Reasons for Failure in Witnessing

1. No plan   2. Fear of men

A Plan

Your message must include the following four
parts. The manner of presentation may vary.
With some people you may need to spend more
time on one part than you do with others. It
is important that you have a plan so you can present the Gospel without wandering or getting
sidetracked, and it will help you to control the
conversation.

1. *The Fact and Penalty of Sin*

"For all have sinned, and come short of the
glory of God" (Romans 3:23). "For the wages
of sin is death" (Romans 6:23).

The person you are witnessing to must realize
that he is a sinner and lost, or he will not see his
need for a Saviour. The penalty must be paid,
either by each individual or by someone else
(Ezekiel 18:4; Romans 5:12; Galatians 3:10;
Hebrews 9:27).

He must realize he needs to be saved.

2. *A Free Gift*

"But the gift of God is eternal life through Jesus Christ our Lord" (Romans 6:23). "Not by works of righteosuness which we have done, but according to his *mercy* he saved us" (Titus 3:5). "For by grace are ye saved through faith; and that not of yourselves: it is the *gift* of God: Not of *works,* lest any man should boast" (Ephesians 2:8, 9).

He must realize he cannot save himself.

3. *Christ Paid the Penalty*

"Who his own self bare our sins in his own body on the tree, that we, being dead to sins, should live unto righteousness: by whose stripes ye were healed" (I Peter 2:24). He was our Substitute. "For Christ also hath once suffered for sins, the just for the unjust, that he might bring us to God" (I Peter 3:18). "For Christ hath redeemed us from the curse of the law, being made a curse for us" (Galatians 3:13; Isaiah 53:6; Romans 5:8; II Corinthians 5:21).

Only Christ could pay the penalty for someone else, because He is the only Person who had no sin (I Peter 2:22). He could redeem all mankind because He is worth more than all the people who have ever lived.

He must understand that Christ has provided salvation for him.

4. *Must Believe and Receive Him as Saviour*

Jesus said: "Behold, I stand at the door, and knock: if *any man* hear my voice, and open the door, I *will come in* to him" (Revelation 3:20). "But as many as received him, to them gave he power to become the sons of God, even to them that believe on his name" (John 1:12).

A doctor can prescribe the medicine you need when sick, but if you do not take it it will not do any good. You can sincerely believe that the medicine is good; you can even understand how it is made and how it will work in your body; hold it in your hand and admire it; but it will not help until you take it. Many people know many things about Jesus, His life and death and resurrection, but they have never received Him as their own personal Saviour.

He must receive Jesus as his personal Saviour.

If he does this, God says he has everlasting life. Have him read John 3:16; 5:24; I John 5:11-13. God wants him to know that he is saved.

Do's in Telling the Message:

Do try to talk to the person alone.

Do use your Bible after you get started. Try to get him to read the verses himself.

Do try to get a decision. If you feel he is under conviction try to get him to kneel and pray with you. (No salesman would present his product without giving you a chance to buy it.) Remember, however, that the new birth is a work of the Holy Spirit.

Do make sure he clearly understands how to receive the Saviour, so if he does not do it in your presence he can later by himself.

DON'TS IN TELLING THE MESSAGE:

Don't use big words and theological phrases. Keep it simple.

Don't be led off the subject to some side issue or catch question.

Don't be afraid to say, "I do not know." But do not stop; tell what you *do* know; what Jesus has done for you. Raising difficult questions is only Satan's trick.

Don't argue.

Don't become discouraged. Profit by your mistakes.

THE APPROACH

Perhaps the hardest part of witnessing is getting started. How can you approach someone and bring the conversation around to spiritual things without being rude?

"The fear of man bringeth a snare" (Proverbs 29:25). Pray for boldness (Acts 4:29, 31).

Moses said: "I am not eloquent . . . I am slow of speech, and of a slow tongue. And the Lord said unto him, Who hath made man's mouth? . . . have not I the Lord? Now therefore go, and I will be with thy mouth, and teach thee what thou shalt say" (Exodus 4:10-12).

Pray for God to open the door if He wants you to talk to a certain person. Then look for common interests, or something for which you can sincerely commend him. Do not use flattery. Someone once said that it is not so much what we say as how we say it (II Timothy 2:24, 25).

If the person does not want to talk to you, or he gets angry or changes the subject, perhaps this is not the time or the Lord does not want you to witness to him. You must be sensitive to the Holy Spirit's guidance; He is Lord of the harvest. Let Him direct you to where the crop is waiting to be harvested, or to where the fish are biting.

METHODS OF TURNING A CONVERSATION TO SPIRITUAL SUBJECTS—

1. *Occupational method—*

A carpenter—I have a Friend who was a carpenter. Jesus must have worked many years with

Joseph before beginning His ministry. What kind of a house are you building? Is it on the rock which is Christ (Matthew 7:24-27)?

A bookkeeper—Talk about the books God is keeping.

A barber—Have you ever cut several pounds of hair from one person's head?

(Story of Absalom in II Samuel 14:26; 200 shekels. Perhaps two weights, among Israelites called a shekel, one lighter, one heavier—one-sixtieth of a pound and/or twice that weight.)

2. *Miracle method*—Talk about a miracle of nature and the God who made it possible.

3. *Object method*—Use some object close at hand.

Water—tell about the *living water* Jesus promised.

Pencil eraser—tell how we all make mistakes but God has provided a way to *erase* our sins.

Gospel coin—with your change carry a coin that has a verse on each side.

Tracts—give an attractively printed tract. Say you would like to have him read it when he has time. (Do not expect him to stand right there and read it.) In this case you are just using it as an opening; then go on talking to him if he is receptive.

Newspaper—almost every newspaper will have one or more stories that can be used to turn thoughts to the future life.

4. *The question method*—The use of a thought-provoking question. With the proper tact this

can be a very effective method. People like to tell what they know, or give their opinion, so let them talk.

SAMPLE QUESTIONS—

1. Do you ever read the Bible?
2. Will you please tell me what this verse means?
3. Do you ever go to church?
4. How does God save a sinner?
5. Can you tell me the way to Heaven?
6. Upon what do you base your hope of Heaven?
7. Can you know for certain where you will spend the next life?
8. How many sins are against you to date?
9. Are you bad enough to go to Hell?
10. Are you good enough to go to Heaven?
11. What excuse will you make to God?
12. Why should God take you to Heaven?
13. Can you tell me how to be saved?
14. When did you receive eternal life?
15. Are you interested in spiritual things?
16. Have you ever thought of becoming a Christian?
17. May I tell you about something that has meant more to me than anything else in my life?

Sometimes it is better to put the question in the third person as though someone else had asked it. "If someone would ask you, 'What is a Christian?' what would you say?" (If you use this question be sure to point out that a Christian is not someone who does certain things, but someone who has met and received the Lord Jesus as Saviour.)

FIND OUT AS SOON AS POSSIBLE WHERE HE
     STANDS—

Be a good listener.

Ask questions. Do not be too eager to talk,
but do guide the conversation.

Watch his face, observe his tone and manner.
Make sure he is not acting or putting up a front.
The Holy Spirit will sometimes reveal to you
his true position. *It is wrong to take someone's
salvation for granted.*

All sinners need to understand the four parts
of the Gospel message already given, but there
are some attitudes and excuses for which the following verses will be helpful:

1. The self-righteous—Isaiah 64:6; Galatians
    2:21; 3:10; Titus 3:5; James 2:10.
2. The defiant in unbelief—John 5:39, 40.
    The defiant in wickedness—Luke 6:45;
    Romans 1:28-32; 3:4, 5.
3. I cannot hold out—John 10:28, 29; I Peter
    1:5.
4. I cannot understand the Bible—I Corin-
    thians 2:14; II Corinthians 4:3.
5. I am too great a sinner—John 6:37; Ro-
    mans 5:8; I Timothy 1:15.
6. Too many hypocrites in the church—Ro-
    mans 2:4, 5; 14:12.
7. One cannot be sure of salvation—I John
    5:10-13.
8. I have my own idea about how to be saved
    —Proverbs 14:12; Jeremiah 17:9; Acts
    4:12.

9. I do not feel ready—Joshua 24:15; Proverbs 27:1; 29:1; II Corinthians 6:2; Hebrews 2:1-3.
10. The worldly wise—Isaiah 1:18; Matthew 18:3, 4.
11. The indifferent—Mark 8:36; John 3:18; Romans 2:12.
12. I am not too bad—John 3:3.

There is an answer in the Bible for every excuse man can offer.

Try to keep to the main message of the Gospel and answer questions later, if at all possible.

PRACTICE

Many people are afraid of the sound of their own voices. Practice with your prayer partner, your husband or wife, or some other member of your family. Act as though the individual is earnestly seeking help, and go over the four parts of the Gospel message using your Bible. Sometimes have the person read the verses; and sometimes act as if you were without your Bible. (Older people often have trouble reading the small print of a Bible, or you might witness to someone who could not read.)

Let the one who is acting as the seeker give some of the most common excuses. Practice meeting him with the Scripture verses and turning the conversation back to his decision. Let him ask or bring up topics (differences in denominations, ordinances, rituals, etc.) to lead you away from your Gospel message.

Usually the best way to handle something like this would be, "I have my own beliefs about what the Bible teaches, but the first thing necessary is to receive Jesus as your Saviour." Or "I will try to explain that later, but first I would like to finish telling you about this." Or "It is important that every Christian become associated with a local church, but that is the second step. First you need to become a Christian. Then God will help guide you in deciding which local church to join." There are some questions you will have to meet and answer that are a real problem to the person. Meet them and then go back to your message.

Do not be afraid of honest problems. The person will appreciate your interest in him and be much more receptive. Sometimes an honest "I don't know but will try to find out" is the wisest thing you can say. Then tell what you do know, the Gospel.

Practice giving your personal testimony—how you came to know the Lord and how He has met the need in your life. Be sure to use Scripture verses in it. For example, "Then I realized as the Bible says, 'the wages of sin is death' and that I was lost." Or "Then I understood what the verse meant when it said, 'For Christ also hath once suffered for sins, the just for the unjust.' " In this type of witnessing it is important to have all your verses memorized. This type of witnessing is very effective and almost always courteously received. The person does not feel preached at, but will hear how Christ has saved you and changed your life.

Now get started.

MEMORY HELPS

You will find the verses you have committed to memory very valuable as you witness to others. Listed below are 20 of the most important verses. You may want to add others. We have assigned seven. This is your *fishing tackle.*

Assignment:	Extra tackle:
1. The fact and penalty of sin Romans 3:23 Romans 6:23	Proverbs 14:14; John 3:8; Romans 2:12; Romans 5:12; Romans 14:12; Galatians 3:10; Hebrews 9:27; Revelation 21:8
2. A free gift Ephesians 2:8, 9	Titus 3:5
3. Christ has paid the penalty Galatians 3:13 I Peter 2:24	II Corinthians 5:21; I Peter 3:18
4. Must believe and receive Him as Saviour John 1:12 Revelation 3:20	John 3:3; John 5:24

Be sure to learn the references so you can find them quickly when needed.

QUESTIONS

1. Only preachers and missionaries should
   be able to witness for Christ (I Peter T F
   3:15). □ □

2. Take the message

   □ Mark 16:15 (a) to the uttermost part
                     of the earth
                 (b) to every creature
   □ Acts 1:8   (c) because we are not
                     ashamed of the Gos-
   □ Rom. 1:16   pel, for it is the power
                     of God unto salvation

3. Romans 10:17 teaches faith comes by
   □ the Word of God
   □ practicing
   □ being baptized

4. What is the seed by which people are "born-
   again" (I Peter 1:23)? _____

5. Who also has a part in the new birth (John
   3:16)? _____

6. The Bible teaches in John 14:6 that all T F
   religions lead to Heaven. □ □

7. An idol worshiper can be saved by his sincere
   attitude (Prov. 14:12; Acts 4:12; Rom. 1:20;
   2:12-16; I Cor. 10:20). _____

8. How many different kinds of sinners are named
   in Rev. 21:8? _____ Are liars included in
   this list? _____ Do you know anyone who
   has not told at least one lie? _____ Do
   you believe Ezek. 18:4? _____ Does everyone need a Saviour? _____

9. What main points of the message must be understood?

   Rom. 3:23 _____

   Rom. 6:23a _____

   Rom. 6:23b _____

   Gal. 3:13 _____

   John 1:12 _____

   I John 5:11-13 _____

10. Besides a lack of knowledge of the Bible, Christians often fail to witness because they are afraid (Prov. 29:25).   T F ☐ ☐

11. To help you witness more effectively, you should pray for

    ☐ Acts 4:29, 31   (a) compassion

    ☐ Matt. 9:36   (b) wisdom

                      (c) boldness

    ☐ Eph. 6:19   (d) the utterance, or

    ☐ James 1:5   words to speak

12. Should you ever argue when trying to witness to someone? _____

13. Write out your own testimony briefly so you can give it in five minutes or less. Remember to include the Gospel; *it* is the power of God.

14. Will you pray that God will allow you to witness for Him in the next 24 hours? _____ Will you go one step farther and pray your witness will bear fruit and God will allow you to lead someone to Christ in the next 24 hours? _____ If so, remember everyone you meet may be *the one*. Do not try to look for "likely candidates" but seek to courteously approach each one until the Holy Spirit opens the door for you; then introduce that one to Christ.

15. If for some reason you fail to find someone to whom you can witness, will you write a letter to an unsaved acquaintance giving your testimony, what Christ means to you? _____

Have you memorized the assigned verses (the *fishing tackle*)? _____ How many extra blessings? _____ How many *quiet times* this week? _____ How many chapters in your Bible? _____

SPIRITUAL CHILD CARE

FOLLOW-UP

The Lord told His disciples not only to preach the Gospel to every creature, but also "teaching them to observe all things whatsoever I have commanded you" (Matthew 28:20). It was not His desire that they should be won to Him and then forgotten.

We have termed this spiritual child care as *follow-up*. Its aim is to help the new "babe in Christ" grow into a happy, mature Christian, who in turn will go out and lead other souls to Christ and help them grow into spiritual maturity.

WHERE DO THE NEW CHRISTIANS COME FROM?

Most of the new Christians will come from the following three groups:

1. United evangelistic crusades
2. Local church program or evangelistic meetings
3. Personal evangelism by individuals

There are always a certain number of people who move into your community and transfer their membership from another local church. This is sometimes an opportune time to interest them in studying the Bible. Many have come to know the Lord months or even years before but never have grown spiritually, even though they might have been quite active in another church.

Needs

Each new Christian has certain definite needs. These are discussed in Lesson 2.

They are needed immediately. Satan will not wait until Sunday to attack.

Although there are certain things every new Christian needs to know, there are also individual needs, problems, and questions for which he must have the answers. Each new Christian is a little different than the last one.

The Death Rate

What would you do or think if you lived in a community where 400 out of every 1,000 babies were born dead? Where 300 of these 600 perished as babies; where of the remaining 200 only 25 lived to be teenagers; and of the 25 teenagers only 5 lived to be adults, get married, and have children of their own? You would be very concerned. You would try to find something to help the situation.

Although it will vary over different parts of the country, according to a recent survey about 60 per cent of the people now profess to belong to some church. This, of course, includes every kind and variety of organization and cult that affiliates itself with the name of Christ. We realize that a large portion of the "members" of these groups are unsaved, but for this illustration we shall consider them as "real" Christians.

If you think of the 1,000 people that live closest to you, your neighbors, friends and acquaintances, 40 per cent of them are spiritually dead, lost without Christ. Of the 600 who will join churches in their lifetime only about 200 will grow spiritually.

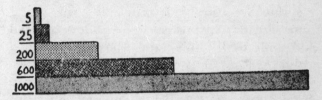

Many will not even have the assurance that they are saved, never learn to study their Bibles, never pray except when they are in trouble, and in five years after "joining" will not attend regularly. This will hold true of anyone old enough to make his own decision as to whether he goes or stays at home. Children are often forced to go against their will.

HELPERS

Of the 200 people found in the average church on a Sunday morning, about 25 will be carrying almost all the load. The rest of the people will help a little here and there, but they are not the kind the pastor can depend upon. Among the working 25 will be some who are not to be classed as spiritual workers, but are helping out in the church program just as they do in civic organizations and clubs. After a year or so they will tire of it and quit, even though they are sincere. Their work can only be classified as works of the "flesh."

REAL WORKERS

Out of the 25 will be about 5 people who could be classified as spiritual Christians—people who have a strong devotional life, who spend time each day in prayer, and who love to read and study their Bibles, and who are concerned about the lost. They are Christians who, by personal witnessing, are leading others to Christ. On any given Sunday in the average church of 200 members it would be unusual to find more than 5 people who would come under this classification. Many pastors could not find one. What is the trouble? Is being a happy, fruitful, spiritual Christian beyond the reach of the average person? It was not in New Testament days. Why are there not more converts growing into mature, spiritual, soul-winning Christians? Do you want the souls the Lord gives you to remain "babes"?

NO SPIRITUAL CHILD CARE

The big reason that most Christians remain "babes in Christ" is that they have not been given the spiritual child care they needed. They have not been taught the basic principles of the Christian life. Children are taught to feed themselves, to wash and dress, to read and write and are given twelve or more years of schooling and then trained for a particular job or occupation.

THE AVERAGE FOLLOW-UP PROGRAM

The normal thing in a church is to introduce the new "babe" to all the people, perhaps even bring him a time or two in your own car, and then find a job in the church program and put him to work. The new job is often just "busy work." This does not help him to grow, but just makes him tired and he may stop coming except when his conscience bothers him or he is in trouble. If he keeps coming, in a year or so he is considered a mature Christian, capable of most any job in the church if he can pray in public and give a talk.

TRAINING

If analyzed his training would consist of 25 hours of lessons in a Sunday school class (often much of this time is taken up by class business), perhaps the same amount of time or a little more of sermons by the pastor, maybe 10 hours of reading the Bible on his own, a few fellowship meetings, and he is supposed to be a good Christian. In some churches he may have 10 or 12 hours in a new-member class, studying church creeds and government or even have memorized a catechism, but no effort has been made to understand or meet his real spiritual needs.

Sunday school, training union, preaching service, or a new-member class cannot do a good job of follow-up. In any of these the lessons must change. The same things cannot be taught each week, but a new Christian needs first things first. He cannot wait weeks for a new class to start, or he might be too timid to ask questions in a class. Each of these classes and organizations have their own purpose, but they are not what a brand-new "babe" in Christ needs to start on the road to Christ-likeness. They will all supplement and speed up his growth later, but he must get started right first.

REASONS THAT DEMAND INDIVIDUAL FOLLOW-UP

1. *Different Religious Backgrounds*

One person may have attended a good Bible-believing Sunday school and church for years, another a modernistic church; another may have been mixed up in some cult; and the next one may have had no religious training of any kind.

2. *Different Educational Backgrounds*

One person may be a college graduate, the next an eighth-grade graduate, the next unable to even write his name. But they all need to grow in the Lord and they can if given the proper attention.

3. *Different Ages and Sexes*

The first new convert may be a teenager, but

the next may be a grandmother, and the next a businessman.

4. *Different Home Life*

There is a big difference in the problems that arise in a Christian home and in a home where one of the mates or both parents are unsaved. Divorce and remarriage pose their problems. In-laws sometimes add to the confusion. Sickness in the home and many other things can hinder or pose special problems in the life of a new Christian.

5. *Different Occupations*

Having to work with godless associates or employers often poses a problem. Some jobs may be of a questionable nature or not too ethical. Some jobs are more physically exhausting than others. Sunday work may be required, or evening or night shift, making church attendance difficult, impractical or impossible.

6. *Different Amounts of Free Time*

Some people have many more responsibilities than others and will be able to spend less time studying.

7. *Different Hobbies and Recreational Habits*

Television is one of the most time-consuming methods of relaxation today. Some people have become almost enslaved to it. Others may have the habit of playing golf, or going fishing, or working in the yard, or just sleeping on Sunday morning.

If the teaching is attempted in a class, all of these factors make it impossible to meet the needs of an individual except in a general way. If someone is absent this complicates the problem even more.

8. *Different Degrees of Interest*

There must be a desire to grow. Some new Christians are hungry for the Word. They should be helped and allowed to grow as fast as possible. Others soon lose their interest. Even though we would like to see all become fruitful Christians, every one will not, but the percentage should be raised as high as possible. Some will show a marked disinterest in Bible study. This might be hard to understand unless it is realized that all decisions for Christ are not genuine. Some may have been awakened to their need, perhaps have the head knowledge but never have applied it to their hearts. Rather than help deceive them by putting on the garments of church membership, baptism and good works, individual follow-up will often lead an awakened sinner into a real acceptance of Christ as Saviour.

What Is the Solution?

A flexible program administered whenever possible individually, person to person, to meet the individual need. This course has been written in an attempt to meet that need.

An attempt has been made to include all the essential things *every* new Christian needs to know to mature spiritually. Several methods are suggested to get the job done. The material is presented in book form, and one chapter at a time should be assigned to prevent hurried sampling of the material without really applying it to the life.

By working with each person individually you are able to help *when* he needs it most. Follow-up should start thirty seconds after the soul winner is convinced the one with whom he is working has received Jesus as Saviour.

The Bible course has been designed with optional features which will allow those who are really "hungry" for the Word, or those who have more free time, to go through the lessons more thoroughly. The rate of study can be adjusted to each person's ability and time available.

THREE WAYS OF USING THE BIBLE COURSE—

1. *Through a Church's New-Member Department*

All new converts and membership transfers are assigned to a counselor. The counselor meets with the new Christian and goes over his answers with him, tries to help with his problems, answers his questions and then assigns the next lesson. The counselor then turns in a regular progress report to the church office.

2. *By the Individual Soul Winner*

Many churches do not have a follow-up program of any kind. Perhaps the Lord has allowed you the privilege of leading a soul to Him, and you would like to help him grow. The only difference now will be that you assume the responsibility of getting the Bible course and turn in reports only to the Lord. If you yourself have finished the course you can help the next person. You do not have to be an expert, and you will both grow spiritually as you study together. It might surprise you how much more you will learn the second time.

3. *By Correspondence*

There are some new converts who will move out of the community so you cannot have further personal contact. Souls won while traveling, boys going to the Armed Forces, and others of this type are hard to help. For this reason, if possible, try to interest them in studying by correspondence. This can be done on an individual basis or through a church.

PREPARATION OF THE COUNSELOR

If you have faithfully studied the lessons, have had your *quiet time,* and have hidden the Word in your heart, you can help a new Christian learn to do the same.

T. L. C.—TENDER LOVE AND CARE

These are the main ingredients in your relations with the one you are counseling. "And the servant of the Lord must not strive; but be gentle unto all men, apt to teach, patient" (II Timothy 2:24). "But we were gentle among you, even as a nurse cherisheth her children. . . .

As ye know how we exhorted and comforted and charged every one of you, as a father doth his children" (I Thessalonians 2:7, 11).

How to Start

As soon as you are convinced that the person to whom you are witnessing has received Christ as Saviour start your follow-up work. First, you want him to understand he now has eternal life and God wants him to know that he does. Have him read I John 5:11-13. Ask if he meant what he said when he asked Jesus to come into his heart as his Saviour. If he says, "Of course I meant it," or something like that, ask him what it was Jesus promised to do in Revelation 3:20. Then ask, "If Christ said He would come in and you ask Him to come in, is He there?" Then "If Jesus came into your heart, what do these verses (I John 5:11-13) say you have?" You want the person to believe Christ has saved him because God has *promised* it in His Word.

Another pitfall is he may trust in feelings. Satan will try to cause him to doubt that he is saved and will probably work through feelings.

Give him another verse so he will know it will not be through his own strength, but that God will keep him for His own. John 10:27, 28 are good verses to use.

Leave Something with Him

You will have told him many things and his mind will be in a whirl. The Gospel of John arranged by T. C. Horton and printed by Moody

Press is excellent for this purpose. It presents God's plan for the salvation of a sinner. This will give the person a chance to go over it again alone. It also has a place in the front for him to sign his name, recording the fact that he has received Christ as Saviour. Have him date it so he will know the date of his second birthday. Explain that it is similar to the Gospel in his Bible with verses underlined for emphasis. Ask him to read at least the first three chapters that night.

What Is Next? Pray—

The new convert needs your prayers. This is one of the most critical times in his Christian life. Pray daily. Paul's prayer for the Colossians is a good example. (Read Colossians 1:9-11.)

Call Back—

In the next twenty-four hours try to see him again. Satan will have attacked him in all his fury. If it is impossible to see him, try to call him on the telephone, or write a short letter. In your first call, if conditions are favorable, tell him you would like to show him something that meant a great deal in your life. If he is watching a favorite TV program, has company, is getting ready to go somewhere or is otherwise occupied, make a definite date to visit him later. Do not show him what you have. Keep him in suspense. Try to get him to understand that the Christian life should be the happiest life possible on this earth, and that the Bible has many wonderful things in it, but that each new Christian is born as a *"babe* in Christ." Your personal testimony and enthusiasm will be very important.

THE LESSON

Open the new copy of the Bible course and explain that it has been written especially for new Christians, to answer their questions, and to meet their needs.

Go over the first lesson with him. Look up the references, then tell him you want to leave it with him and have him do the second one by himself. Do not try to get him to say that he will do all twelve lessons; just this one now. Make a definite date to come back and see him. You might preview the lesson by mentioning the importance and use of the four memory verses.

WARNING!

1. Watch your personal appearance, and be careful that you don't have bad breath.
2. Don't teach with a "know-it-all" attitude, but rather from a sharing attitude with each one contributing.
3. Don't argue, and try to avoid controversial questions and denominational issues.
4. Don't try to teach too fast. This is all new to him.

5. Watch that you don't spend too much time just because he is a good listener. Don't give him too much; spiritual *babes* can get indigestion too.

6. Don't get sidetracked. Stay with the lesson. Try to answer any questions that are a real problem to him but put the others down on his list for future study.

7. Be observant; take nothing for granted. Notice what he says about people and things, his prayer requests, and other interests (Proverbs 27:23).

8. Go over each of the following lesson plans by yourself before you try to help with his lesson. In this way you can get his needs and the aim of the lesson firmly in mind before you meet him.

LESSON 1. MEETING CHRIST

Needs: To be saved.

Aim: To make sure his decision is genuine; that he has really been "born again."

Difficulties: Satan has blinded him.

Steps: Make the personal application of the salvation verses to himself—

  To receive Jesus as Saviour

  To thank God for saving him

  Tell his friends about it

Suggestions:

Use question 24 as an opportunity to pray with him. Make it short, encourage him to pray, and try to make this a regular part of meeting together.

In each lesson there are steps the new Christian should be encouraged to take. He should not be high-pressured into taking them, or he may not be sincere or may resent it. Emphasize that his decision to receive Jesus was the first of many decisions he must make if he is going to have a happy life.

Your Notes:

LESSON 2. LIFE HAS BEGUN

Needs:

    To feel safe
    Some verses to meet the attacks of Satan
    To start studying the Bible
    Christian fellowship
    To realize he is a spiritual *babe*

Aims:

    Show the way to meet Satan is with the Word
    That his life should be different now
    That he can live a happy *abundant life*
    That God is good and will take care of him

Difficulties:

 Old habits and friends

 Thinks he is too busy to study

 Not seeing the importance of the memory
  work

 Thinking he is not able to memorize

Steps:

 1. To read the Bible each day

 2. Go to church next Sunday

 3. Start a reading record

 4. Memorize the four verses this week

 5. Finish the first two lessons this week

Suggestions:

If he thinks he cannot memorize, ask him what his address is, his telephone number, questions about his hobby or job that involves a lot of memory work, until he realizes that he can and does memorize many things. Give him your testimony—how much it has meant to you. Let him check you on the verses.

 Ask him to go to church with you.

 Check his Bible-reading record.

 Get him in contact with other Christians, and Christian groups.

Your Notes:

Lesson 3. Learning to Eat

Needs:

To understand the conflict going on in his heart

To know the power for Christian living is the Holy Spirit

The Holy Spirit is a Person not a thing

The Holy Spirit is present in his heart

That he grows through the Word

Aims:

Explain the dual nature

Help him understand about the Holy Spirit's place in his life.

Show him how to feed on the Word

Set some goals

Difficulties:

Want to skip around in the Bible

Cannot understand parts of the Bible

Putting things off

Steps:

Start a future study and memory list

Memorize four verses

Suggestions:

Ask what he is learning in his reading, or what particular blessing he has received from the Word recently. Share some of your blessings with him.

Your Notes:

LESSON 4. LEARNING TO TALK

Needs:

The privilege and power of prayer
How to pray
What he can pray for
Watch God answer definite prayer requests

Aims:

Show the necessity for balance between prayer
and the Word
Show the power of prayer and God's faithfulness
Establish good prayer habits

Difficulties:

Afraid or embarrassed to pray with others
Try to imitate phrases of other people
Be vague in requests (Bless so-and-so, and so-
and-so, help so-and-so, etc.)

Steps:

Start a prayer list of unsaved friends
Prayer before meals
Memory verses

Suggestions:

Share prayer requests with each other. Tell
him how God has answered prayer for you.

Your Notes:

LESSON 5. STARTING TO WALK

Needs:

To understand what the Holy Spirit can do
for him

How to be filled with the Holy Spirit and stay
filled

Aims:

Show that this is the happy life
The only way to please God
The only way God can really use him

Difficulties:

Afraid he is giving up too much and will be
unhappy

Afraid God will ask him to do some hard
thing

Steps:

Yield to God and be filled by the Holy Spirit
Memory verses

Suggestions:

Your personal testimony will help more than
almost anything else. If he does not yield himself to God he will never grow or be used very
much by God.

Your Notes:

LESSON 6. WALKING WITHOUT STUMBLING

Needs:

    To know that temptations will come
    How they will come
    How to meet them
    He can be victorious

Aims:

    To show God's faithfulness
    How to be victorious
    Help him know his own weaknesses

Difficulties:

    Overconfident
    Careless

Steps:

    List the desires Satan might use to tempt
        For his own personal use.)
    Memory verses

Suggestions:

Do not try to make the new Christian think you have conquered all your problems and that Satan does not bother you any more, or that you never have temptations.

Your Notes:

Lesson 7. Washing and Spanking

Needs:

How to get right with God if he sins
That God disciplines rebellious children

Aims:

Understand what confession means
He cannot play with sin
How to avoid chastisement

Difficulties:

Satan causes him to doubt his forgiveness
Excuses for sinning
Not wanting to admit sin, pride
Not recognizing God's chastening

Steps:

Make a list for his own use of every one who
has wronged him, and then one by one go
through the list and forgive them.
Memory verses

Suggestions:

Many Christians limit their usefulness because
of the unforgiveness and grudges they harbor in
their hearts.

Your Notes:

Lesson 8. Enjoying the Family

Needs:

Fellowship with others
How to select a local church
Understand what composes the Body of Christ

Aims:

Show the need for fellowship
The need for local church membership
Guidance in picking a local church

Difficulties:

Too many kinds of churches
Prejudiced about church membership or certain denominations because of family traditions
Not understanding God's program for the church
Bashful about meeting people

Steps:

A prayer partner
Family devotions
Local church membership
Memory verses

Suggestions:

Take him with you to church. If he has not been in church before, explain the order of the service so he will know what is going on and what to do. Avoid embarrassing him.

Your Notes:

Lesson 9. Growing Through Fellowship with God

Needs:

To know Christ as a Person
Develop a strong devotional life

Aims:

Establish a *quiet time*
How to use the Word to search his heart
Encourage him to make definite applications
   to his life

Difficulties:

Thinking of God as away off somewhere
Too busy
Too lazy
No definite schedule for a quiet time

Steps:

Start a quiet time
Memory verses

Suggestions:

Tell how and where you have your quiet time;
how you solved some of your problems, such as
going to sleep, wandering thoughts, etc.

Your Notes:

LESSON 10. FOLLOWING DIRECTIONS

Needs:

Guidance for daily living

Guidance in choosing life's vocation

Aims:

To show the promises of guidance

To show the sources of guidance

Methods of determining the will of God

Difficulties:

Differences in man's standards of holiness

Prejudiced thinking

Self-will

Lure of the world

Steps:

Start a prayer list

Start praying for guidance for the place and way in which God would have him serve in His harvest field

Memory verses

Suggestions:

Help him gather and list information concerning the different fields of service, so you can pray about it together. Get down to business; do not just daydream.

Your Notes:

LESSON 11. FISHING

Needs:

How to witness
How to open the conversation
His responsibility to the world
Witnessing must be Spirit-directed and Spirit-empowered

Aims:

How to lead a person to Christ
How to start
To help understand what the Gospel is
How to meet excuses with the Bible

Difficulties:

The fear of man
Lack of knowledge of the Bible
Afraid of the sound of his own voice
Excuses and trick questions
No plan

Steps:

Write out his personal testimony
Practice with someone
Pray for a chance to witness every 24 hours
Memorize verses

Suggestions:

Take the new Christian with you; let him hear you witness.

Your Notes:

LESSON 12. SPIRITUAL CHILD CARE
T.L.C.—tender love and care

Reasons for Failure:

Not enough prayer
Not done lovingly
Not done watchfully
Not done person to person
Not the example you should be
Discouragement
Seeking self-glory
Too busy to do it right
Driving instead of leading
Letting him get involved in a church program
    too soon
Get too busy and stop studying

YOU MUST REALIZE—

Everyone you lead to the Lord will not start these lessons. Everyone who starts will not finish. Everyone who finishes will not do all the work recommended. Do not be discouraged. The average now is not more than one mature soul-winning Christian out of every 120 professing church members. If we could only get one new Christian out of every 10 to spiritual maturity

we would increase the spiritual effectiveness of the church twelve times. It would be hard to estimate this effect on the rest of the church, and those who start and only go part way through the lessons.

QUESTIONS

1. A good soldier of Christ should not become entangled with the affairs of this life (II Tim. 2:4).

   T □ F □

2. Follow-up work is best done in a class.

   T □ F □

3. What characteristics must a good servant of the Lord have according to II Tim. 2:24?
   □ not strive, be gentle, apt to teach, patient
   □ strong, powerful in prayer, alert
   □ a good example, wise, sincere

4. Follow-up work should begin
   □ the first Sunday after people are saved
   □ as soon as a class can be organized
   □ as soon as they are saved

5. Most Christians grow into mature, useful, witnessing Christians.

   T □ F □

6. Good follow-up will sometimes reveal that the new member has not fully understood the Gospel nor made a real decision for Christ.

   T □ F □

7. Paul's prayer in Colossians 1:9-11 is a good example of the things for which we should ask the Lord on behalf of a new Christian.

   T □ F □

8. The example the counselor sets is not as   T   F
   important as the things he says.   ☐   ☐

                                      T   F

9. Most people like to memorize.   ☐   ☐

10. The counselor should be observant and   T   F
    not take things for granted.   ☐   ☐

Have you memorized II Tim. 2:2 _____;
I Peter 2:2-3 _____; Phil. 2:3-4 _____;
Phil. 1:6 _____; Titus 2:12-13? _____
How many extra blessings? _____

11. How many *quiet times* have you had in the
    past week? _____

12. How many chapters have you read since start-
    ing this course? _____

13. Has the Lord given you the privilege of lead-
    ing a soul to Him? _____

14. Have you enjoyed the course? ___ ___

THE FUTURE

The *Abundant Life* Bible Study Course has
introduced you to many interesting subjects of
study. Doubtless there are many things you
would like to understand more fully.

During this course we have tried to help you
establish good spiritual habits—Bible study,
prayer, church attendance, witnessing, etc. The
fruitfulness of your service for God will depend
to a large degree upon your faithfulness in con-
tinuing these things.

There are many subjects which could be recommended for study; the whole Bible is "profit-

able" to you (II Timothy 3:16). Here are a few
—the second coming of Christ, Heaven and Hell,
the Lord's Supper, the creation of the world,
how to rightly divide the Word, covenants of
God, giving, the judgments of God, the parables
of Christ, and the riches of salvation.

We hope by now you are living the *abundant
life* which Christ has promised you. We have
tried to teach you many new things. "Meditate
upon these things; give thyself wholly to them;
that thy profiting may appear unto all" (I Timothy 4:15). Then some day as you stand before
Christ may He say: "Well done, thou good and
faithful servant . . . enter thou into the joy of
thy Lord" (Matthew 25:21).

Moody Press, a ministry of the Moody Bible Institute, is
designed for education, evangelization and edification.
If we may assist you in knowing more about Christ and
the Christian life, please write us without obligation to:
Moody Press, c/o MLM, Chicago, Illinois 60610.